RAVISH THE REPUBLIC

RAVISH THE RE-PUBLIC

THE ARCHIVES OF THE
IRON GARTERS
CRIME/ART COLLECTIVE

BULLETINS,
REPORTS,
EPHEMERA,
PAPER TRAILS,
LETTERS

EDITED AND WRITTEN BY
IRON GARTERS
CO-FOUNDER & SECRETARY

MICHAEL L. BERGER

DEAD LETTER OFFICE, VIA
PUNCTUM BOOKS · BROOKLYN, N.Y.

First published in 2015 by
Dead Letter Office, BABEL Working Group
an imprint of punctum books
Brooklyn, New York
http://punctumbooks.com
http://babelworkinggroup.org

The BABEL Working Group is a collective and desiring-assemblage of scholar-gypsies with no leaders or followers, no top and no bottom, and only a middle. BABEL roams and stalks the ruins of the post-historical university as a multiplicity, a pack, looking for other roaming packs and multiplicities with which to cohabit and build temporary shelters for intellectual vagabonds. We also take in strays.

ISBN-13: 978-0692283950
ISBN-10: 0692283951

Cover Photo: *Rachel, Nevada, near Area 51*, Michael Berger.
Book and cover design: Chris Piuma.

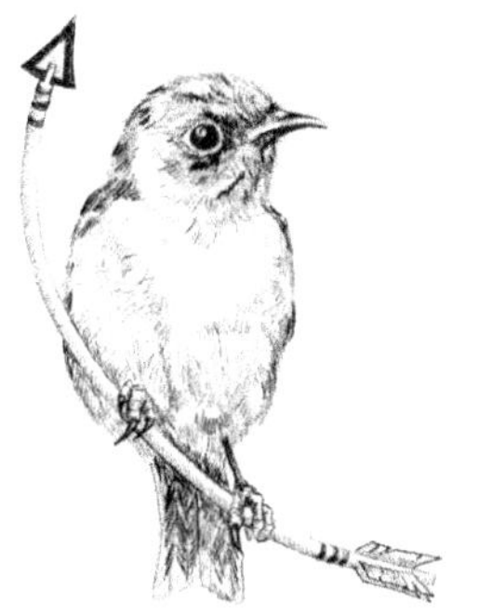

Before you start to read this book,

take this moment to think about making a donation to **punctum books**, an independent non-profit press,

@ http://punctumbooks.com/about/

If you're reading the e-book, you can click on the image below to go directly to our donations site. Any amount, no matter the size, is appreciated and will help us to keep our ship of fools afloat. Contributions from dedicated readers will also help us to keep our commons open and to cultivate new work that can't find a welcoming port elsewhere. Our adventure is not possible without your support.

Vive la open-access.

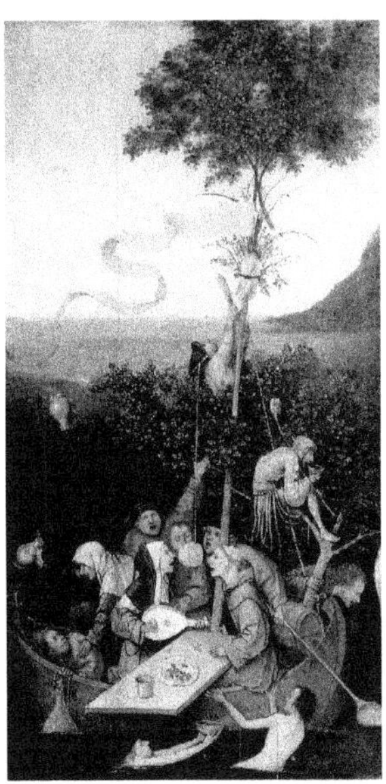

Fig. 1. Hieronymus Bosch, *Ship of Fools* (1490-1500)

TABLE OF CONTENTS

INTRODUCTION

GETTING TO KNOW THE GARTERS

I was a child of a suburban lake, and its scraggly coastline populated by an underground society. That's what I called them when I discovered that "underground" and "subterranean" had exciting insinuations. Words that conjured hiddenness and remoteness, but also the cultivation of secrecy and resistance for their own sake. Surrounding me was the stucco and asphalt and steeples of sun-lit life. But the lake was a dark oasis of unsuspecting thrills. The adrenalized joy of espionage and the catalytic zest of conspiracy: my body wanted these vectors to steer my life. So I read detective and spy fiction, but also delved into the ecstasies of mysticism and theology. All the while I wandered the ragged paths around the water. The human body, I realized, was at the mercy of forces that wanted to use it. The body is a radio for cosmic transmissions! But some of these forces were more beneficial than others. In my receptive imagination, I became a spy for a Goddess in exile, a dethroned and oppressed Sophia who needed my radio-body to help resuscitate her watery kingdom inside the beige and fluorescent compartments of the everyday.

I was lured into the reeds and coves of lacustrine life, but also the ambergris and mildew ambiance of Greyhound stations and empty plazas and seedy motels. Ruinscapes and shadowscapes secreted seductive aromas that lured me away from the bright and sanitized. Wherever shadows fell ornately, where noise became muddied, and wherever human motives turned inconsequential, I gravitated, knowing there was knowledge there in more poetic doses. The opacities within me needed to find their outer world corollaries. Life that seethed and fermented beyond the searchlights of family house and sports field, church and supermarket, Television and youth group: an intricate and suggestive wilderness that, for all the attempts to be dammed and categorized still persevered as an irresistible and mutable Outside. This is the realm of a wild Logos, a savage Gnosis, where Pan, Eros and Dionysus endure, locked in amorous combat, of undomesticated fields in which adventure and transport are still desirable and fruitful endeavors.

As an agent of this underground society, I began to encounter and summon my kindred entities. Whether they were fisherwomen with garter snakes around their arms; or errant lighthouse keepers hunting for crawfish; or soccer stars gone pill-mad and truant; or medicine-mothers leading some scandalous nightlife; or worshippers of minor saints, like Lucia; or bizarre spice importers; or chandelier saboteurs; or textbook redactors; this underground society schemed, muttered, experimented and loved among the reeds and grottoes, gardens and coves, fields and gorges of that sweltering lake district. Their odors and breaths leaked into my room, thru the rattled screen, thru polluted moonlight, thru fig spoor and radio tide. I fell asleep to their coyotes howling in the sage-scrub gullies while the lunar-glazed fig tree rasped the window. Such sounds belied the otherwise suburban, overly-plotted world I lived in; they were goads to more life and more of its *expressing*. To express was something more erotic than telling, more violent, more sensuous, and more complicit in kaleidoscopic erosions and swamp life and the inhuman ecstasy of crows.

I was reading, scribbling, wandering and keeping vigil, gouging minute depths and subtle labyrinths. To be secret was to be apart but also, strangely, to be *in the know*. It was to also be, potentially, forgotten and overlooked, left to your own bizarre and elaborate devices. History was just the history of what has remained or endured as un-secret, or as open secrets. But secret is also a verb, to *secrete*: to take a thing magically outside of yourself as a way to foster connections, alliances, relations, and collaborations. The world, or what little of it I could access was enriched by small, tantalizingly elusive micro-communities that did as little harm as possible but reveled in the adrenalized excitements of their borderland sensualities. They were apart from the legislated spotlights and the gossip mills, but not always; yet they nourished their "apartness" as a sustaining sanctuary to sulk back to when life got overbearing or oppressive.

The Iron Garters Crime/Art Collective was born in the febrile imaginings I made with a few delinquent friends in that wilderness of Southern California. When these friends went their separate ways, I preserved this "underground society" in my own projects as I grew up. When I landed in the dune city of San Francisco, I knew I had reached a place that my imagination had predicated its desires upon. Here artists and alchemists, seekers and sorcerers, "failures" and "outcasts" of all predilections swarmed in crowded, candle-lit apartments while ocean gales shook the rafters. Nightly, complex bacchanalia brought out the most vivid characters into the night; the streets resounded with the discord of souls in ferment, bodies in heat and imaginations unleashed.

Fortified by an education in critical theory and theology, I spent a decade exploring San Francisco (and Oakland) as a place of both self-liberation and self-overcoming, singularly and collectively. Social progress couldn't happen without individual progress; and vice versa; material conditions couldn't improve without alterations in consciousness; and vice versa. Failures and setbacks and instabilities marked much of this era, but also transports and joys and transformative charges into the unknown. In the process I met life-changing collaborators who became, for me, the very blood of the City, especially when the City was at its most imperiled. Daily, we saw our San Francisco over-determined and overrun by the tyrannies of profit, luxury, security and privileged homogeneity masquerading as artisanal variety. We saw this happening in other cities as well: boisterous urban loci that historically are seedbeds of creative ferment and radical resistance were becoming the bedroom-and-restaurant communities of the boringly lucrative and vapidly self-satisfied.

Under these complex conditions, the Iron Garters soldered a compact to resist and sabotage the forces of both inner and outer gentrification, and resisting especially, in Sarah Schulman's words, "the gentrification of the mind." To honor this concord, we knew we would have to make unprecedented collaborations between art and theory, spirituality and labor, crime and love, writing and noise, among other contrasts. The unquestioned divisions between genres and modes and forms could no longer be tolerated. The Academy would have to be thrown into the street. Theory would have to be disrupted by economic brutalities. Culture would have to be rewritten by the powerless. Sexuality and desire would have to be undermined by artistic frenzy and mystical devotion. Above all, we would have to be reckless yet cunning like the most devoted outlaws, protectors of a Wild Outside that has no real analogue in human rationality. The Garters, in deference to those intimations of the lake, agreed to live as smugglers of a precious and sacred ecosystem of wilderness and transport, which they are sworn to protect from all bureaucrats, judges, managers, bankers, zookeepers, cataloguers, economizers, and the rationalistic defangers of culture and vitality.

At the beginning, in the mid-aughts, Garter work had variously provocative manifestations: the cryptic and erotic mail art created in a South of Market office and distributed to special agents; the rowdy theatrical performances hosted by the now-defunct New College of California; the communal, anarchist film screenings at the still-enduring, and always-ramshackle Artists Television Access; as well as the visceral and somatic art work produced by several Feminist and Queer art collectives. Just as powerfully, the Garter ethos extended into and became nourished by the hermetic and pagan communities of San Francisco, many of which proliferated upon the misty hill districts. Suffice to say, despite the economic crimes that were robbing San Francisco of its vitalities, a still vigorous "underground society" endured. And to make sure it still endures the Iron Garters are remobilizing in the imperiled cities of America and beyond as the very threat to progress that insures that the human soul remains imperishable.

The documents that follow are the inaugural and incomplete batch of contagious evidence we have secreted to revive our artistic-criminal lives. A new reader might be confused about our preference for the word, crime. So we ask you to suspend judgment and sink somewhat heedlessly into the heretical counter-histories of creativity and the social. Begin with François Villon, steer into Dada and

'Pataphysics, Genesis P-Orridge's art and music, and then linger long in the Cookie Mueller–era New York of the 1970s. The Iron Garters agree that we are all members of a real criminal organization: Mankind. The Emergency of History is no longer the Exception but the Banality. Therefore, we suggest: embrace the banal by making it, again, theatrical. If the so-called little things are where we might reap the most ardent pleasures, then let's take our own advice and telescope our direst minutiae into ecclesiastical transports. Remember: dominant social strata win out because they have the strongest performers. Bureaucracy and paper trails and red tape are analogues to the complex rituals of a polytheistic society overseen by the most mnemonically gifted of high priests. Organization is always performative, even when it is chaotic.

In that spirit, the Iron Garters are performing a complex criminal and gang-based ritual to exorcise banality and make it again visceral, sensual and immediate. World making is a moment-by-moment process that we cannot ever shirk; and just as often it involves the undoing of one world's parts and fragments to be transposed and reimagined towards the making of another. We are masquerading as criminals only to show you the counter-laws of liberation already inscribed in your cellular makeup. Only when society adopted its hierarchical organization did crime fall into the hands of the powerful and not the playful. Today the criminals wear suffocating suits without anything sexy to hide; when Garters wear suits it's like Christmas wrapping paper around the world's most fetching pair of chainmail lingerie. Garters, thereby, are asked to create their own individual Costumes and Fetishes, Rituals and Rulebooks, Cosmogonies and Charters, Alphabets and Blueprints. Towards this prerogative, we invoke the soul-based writings of neo-Jungian psychologist James Hillman, the artistic/religious letters of performance artist Linda Montano, and the Deleuzian Nomadic Ethics of Rosi Braiddoti, all of whom have acted as "Garter radios," or transmitters of that feral gnosis that belongs to our unhampered bodies and souls.

The Unknown is constantly pinging us for any signs of response no matter how muffled we become by the paranoid dictates of our collective interiority. Does the Unknown come necessarily as Information? Perhaps, and quite often. But to Garters what registers more viscerally as the Unknown arrives as Sensation, which is why our Bodies have become our Crafts, bolstered by souls at their most receptive and vulnerable. We are living in worlds increasingly made insular and corralled by the ejaculation of data. We are corralled by the next update, the next piece of news, the next blip of digital feed as the world our bodies want to play in waits for us outside. Our survival steadily seems to depend on sifting through unquantifiable data. But this is illusory. Sensation contains more knowledge than information, if but we only listened with our whole fleshly, ensouled selves.

When we talk about life, we are only ever talking about strata, ever-shifting, ever-silting layers and strands of existence, like a beach with its tongue in the water, or a swamp with its crotch in the forest. This Garter revelation we owe to two of the most visionary proto-Garters in the theoretical landscape: Gilles Deleuze and Felix Guattari. In league with their findings, Garters love seeking out strategic plateaus among the tumult of entangled boundaries and blurred conditions. There is something about beaches we want to make live in non-beach environments. There is something about the depths that look better when we propel them into the heights. Hierarchies are playgrounds that we can dislodge and reassemble at will, or at caprice. The future belongs to ecologists who can put the Human Bias on the backburner, play with ontological boundaries and create new affiliations that are in the best interest of Life, itself, regardless of anthropocentric desires. What appears ossified to a Non-Garter (that doesn't know s/he is a Garter) is Fluid to a Garter who knows. But all are welcome into the sandbox of knowing, i.e. playing. Ludic Gnosis is for all. The Outside awaits its protectors, its smugglers, its regal feral citizens.

We know that becoming an Iron Garter is a compact of manifold desires buried in each of us, but which has become socialized into docility by the more dominant, more legible social strata. Exiting upon the earth, unfinished at the womb—for all living from the get-go is lavish *unfinishment*—we believe that failure, as the dominant strata recognize and demarcate it, is the only option for us. Failure opens up new worlds of success: it is actually the most fertile, seething realm for all the metamorphoses we define our lives by. The Iron Garters believe that your most brazen and boldest character traits are your most authentic; what you are most apt to suppress for survival and face-saving sake; they are most suited towards vigorous and sincere reality construction, which is a messy yet rewarding job. For Garters, Reality is always Pending. On the same token, what is considered Messy often proves for a Garter to be immensely rewarding. Hence, you must reveal and flex what yearns the hottest in you if you want to make reality.

Reality making is a risky expedition but life is already the riskiest proposition. In order to take the most risks, you have to work in tandem with the riskiest characters, both within and without. This is where leather and chains and nylon can make you feel bolder, can make you perform with a more dynamic devotion to life. This is where dressing as your *drag alter-id* can bolster reality-building confidence. To make reality you must enter into your own visceral personae. The vaudeville chorus you've kept harbored in your heart must come to life. A chorus is a cosmos. So please delight and take initiative from the following paper-trail chorus of the Iron Garters Crime/Art Collective.

Those seeking initiation into the Iron Garters are counseled to write a letter of passionate intent, with a snail-mail address included, to the email: thesaltedlash@gmail.com.

Michael Berger
General Secretary,
Iron Garters Crime/Art Collective
Las Vegas, Nevada
April 13, 2015

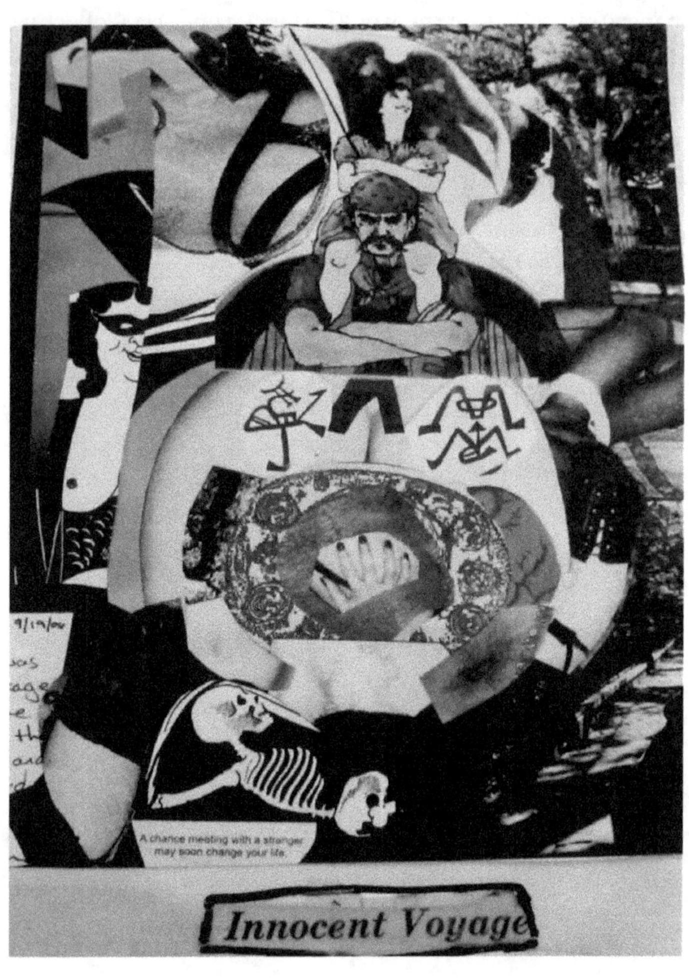
A chance meeting with a stranger may soon change your life.
Innocent Voyage

TWELVE AND ½ THINGS IRON GARTERS KNOW WE NEED NOW

PROPOSALS FOR THE TRANSFIGURATIONS OF SOCIAL & PSYCHIC RELATIONS

1. ***More* Danger, risk, hazard, venture**—our hearts and minds, what's left of them, strewn in *glocal* melee,—but adulterated, banalized, compartmentalized for passive consumptions, incapacitating paranoias, repetition-compulsions and stifling ego-conveniences. These are the political forces constitutive of earth, our newsworthiness, our exemplary losses, our pre-ideological howls, our Heraclitean shit storms, our tabloid spasms. Still we move brutally mediated, inept at energizing, becoming. We *grow* inculcated and fortressed off. Our fears are never ridden out as passages. Nor do we enter into theatrics for healing. So to actualize and imagine: a *craft* that coincides with these fires, fears, fixations. A talismanic way to chaosophize, to live. How is the vessel coextensive with the sea? How is contingency *architechtonic*? Human challenges are not necessarily reasonable ones, so our responses must become extraordinary.

2. **Fiction, poetry, artistry/artfulness, theatrics, in subtle & extreme ubiquities.** How does ART help negotiate/invoke number one (danger)? How can ART build/steer the

craft? How to contrive Chaos, thru ART in advance of Chaos's unspeakable insinuations? How can one make a city out of seductive ploys? For that is the demiurge in the arts: making cities or assemblages, establishing contexts that are radiant and magical and that for the moment eliminate the anxiety of entering them. Most cities now don't.

3. **Knowing: Fiction and Artistry, Theater and Poetry are never really telling lies about us, nor are they ever really telling truths about us; they are doing something else that is not even telling.** Rather, it is *listening:* molecularly assembled of all genera of lies and truths, while also outstripping them, fleeing them, re-fertilizing in the Outside. The earth and stars provide the hints. Listening radiates the Proximity of the Other like nothing else. Art is Play that Animates Matter, to paraphrase Elizabeth Grosz, eminent Deleuzian. And play is not interested in veracity or falsehood, décor or veritas, but rather *Decoverite.*

4. **While Knowing, however that the worst, most destructive lies being told *are* about us.** When the people with the most power tell the biggest lies so that the most people suffer: history. Hence, what are the banal, taken-for-granted relationships between truth and fiction, and how are they used to consolidate power? How can one sabotage such distinctions? Who is an Us? What is a Category good for? Who benefits from its use/abuse? What are the benefits of categories that develop lacunae, trapdoors, embrasures, passages, way stations, hybrid offspring, and tributaries?

5. **The most injurious liars are the ones who speak exclusively in "non-fiction," which is a marketplace term for "truth."** These liars prefer the medium of the report or the

history or the memorandum, to that of the sermon, the essay, the poem, the rant, the novella, the love letter, the erotic comedy, the hermetic pants-splitter and the riddle-song. They prefer a *system* because it gives them something to shove themselves inside of, organs and all: sexual? In its tawdry way, perhaps.

6. **Authenticity and vitality *felt*, especially in the places where they *seem* most absent and where life seems most *spent*.** But the seeming world is an orchestrated world, right? Who makes things *seem*? Who orchestrates my vacillations? What helps us *feel*? Can I *feel* my way to a better-seeming, more pleasurably orchestrated world? How do we reawaken/recognize the *unspent*? Here we establish that ruins are flush with the cosmic continuum, so how can ruins be unspent? And here, again, we turn to the craft.

7. **Nature, or Sex, in terms of the babbling but all-irradiating libidinal substrata of What's Real/This Is.** When Eros comes exploding or streaming or gurgling through us, what do we gain? What do we lose? What if it's a neither force? What are the syllables/symbols/logics for this neither-Eros? If the Panic is Creative, why must we hide from it in Tact and Avoidance? When Eros is no longer Sex but another darker, sulkier, more strident ringing in the trees, what warrens are we lost in? When it articulates as Love, are we saved; if so, why does it *seem* we're never saved? The Garters know no salvations but in energies, Love being one of the Major Ones.

8. **Interminable, intricate, deviant, quite possibly ecstatic/kenotic conversations**—starting with breath/ *pneuma* & words/syllables, eye piercings/loaded looks; and their sincerities, deflections, their crypts and their crafts—

that build "things" on earth. Auden said, "We are on earth to make things"—and he wasn't wrong. Instead of ceaseless and increasingly more futile, self-reflexive "commentary" or the narcissism inherent in our so-called "sharing" economy that dominates/stultifies/petrifies information communities and social media sites, we advise free-feeling and playfully-meandering gifts and exchanges of words, stories, ideas, spells, clues, that become the raw material for physically embodied, person-to-person projects and experiments.

Truthfully, much of what we espouse already happens on the Web, for which we give praise; but too much of what we don't like tends to drown it out.

Remember:
A Gift is *Never* Shared.
A Comment is *Never* an Exchange.
A Conversation is *Always* an Incantation.
A Gift *Becomes Always* a Passage.
(Obsession *Is* a Stadium: Many, Noisy, Consequential)

9. **The *Orgasmic-Enthusiastic* Is *Never* A Terminus, End Point, Destination, Goal, Future Finale, Consolidation—but a chaotically-organizing, perpetually-erotic, rapturous-devotional energy-logic of the Continuous-Fluctuating Present.**

Nobody is done when they come; and coming is never done. Here we leap from Deleuze and Guattari's "plateaus" and "rhizomatics" by way of Gertrude Stein's temporal current of vibrant things, and Virginia Woolf's painstaking molecular attentions, to the nomadic nerve-bibles of Jean Genet and Kathy Acker where the perpetual breakaways of desire, the endless comings (and goings) create unquantifiable intensity-enthusiasm nodes that make cartographies of the present. We also swoon for the art-prayers of Dorothy Iannone and her lifelong search for "Ecstatic Unity," whether through another's Eros, or through her own blood-lantern soul-maps, or even through the wanderings and ordeals and bereavements that constitute a quest for ecstasy in the first place. This is the realm of the Tragic, certainly, but which can be expressed only in Joy, which is far stealthier and more versatile than you expect. Here too, apropos of the Tragic, we enter a world of incredibly injurious economic-driven distortions, where terms like bliss, union, happiness, serenity, harmony and contentment are paraded, parodied and exploited as buyable destinations, panaceas, eternal bunkmates, validating credentials. Our position is simply that life brings no relief, only paths to possibly more exciting, intense, harmonic, loving, galvanizing and pleasurable ways to be unrelieved. And also, not to forget: "Enthusiasm" once meant "taken by divine frenzy, or enraptured by a god" so just as there is no cure for life, there is no room *just* for the individual, for he/she/they/it must contend with the forces that pass through, out of and are already formative of their seemingly isolate subjectivity. So by necessity philosophy enters into inextricable relations with sorcery and the old gods and the Numinous, i.e. The Invisible.

Border work is also bridge work even with wars ongoing inside & out.

10. **New/flexible social *contracts* based on *real* social flux.** Freedom is already a theatrical and ludic proposition that binds us hearts, minds, & props into myriad situations/scenarios with divergent players, many of whom are wildly different than our selves. How can our necessarily incomplete and ever-pending and always-diluted freedoms work and fuse together, i.e. con-tract, to *secrete* new assemblages, forms, imaginaries, encounters? Jean-Luc Nancy's "Being

Singular Plural" is a useful phrase to leap from and out of—right into the music of Richard Hell when he was the first person in New York to wear black jeans.

11. **The Outside.** We grow encumbered by trending stances, the secured positions, the lullabying analyses, the perspectival hair-splittings, the nervousness to *belong*, the hunger to *affiliate*, the tic to *represent*, and the accelerating, repetitive technological Interiority that puppeteers and faux-validates us—but we know it when we feel it, gust of green wind, shore-glass, broken pylons in a quiet field—and it's lost to us, this Outside, inextricably snarled inside where those systems have tyrannized our movements into repeating knots of stifled communication, compromised desire.

12. **The *Sacramental* Approach to Reality.** As criminals, we surprise people, like critics and academics, by advocating tirelessly for this apparent religious tactic; however, many crime-seeking outcasts take "vows" that unite them with the folds of the Outside, among the darkly-grooved forest realms where matter still makes ritual demands of us, where each pinecone resonates like a temple bell, every leaf scintillates in crystalline hints and the oasis we wash our toes in is fed on chthonic shadows. And you'd be surprised by what we mean by criminal too: it's a peculiar and devoted relation with the Outside. It's also romantic realism and the advancements made by *rock n' roll* into the unchecked territory that drove both Jesus and Nietzsche to early deaths.

12½. **The Sacramental Approach to *Irreality, Surreality, Unreality.*** This methodology is explored in our theories, fictions, manifestos, and their oddball bastardizations. Here we entertain a theology of the fragment—in so far as the Whole has been called God, now each fragment is now called god—but also new ways of making sex work in the name of reason. Eros is the ultimate game of fragments become godly. Is this god a criminal, too? It's certainly up for experiment. For more in this vein, consult the works of *'pataphysics*. Consult as well the pending, transmedia fictions of *Noctula*, the mythopoeic ecosystem that keep Garters politically and ethically aroused as they negotiate the more circumscribed grids of the Real.

END BULLETIN

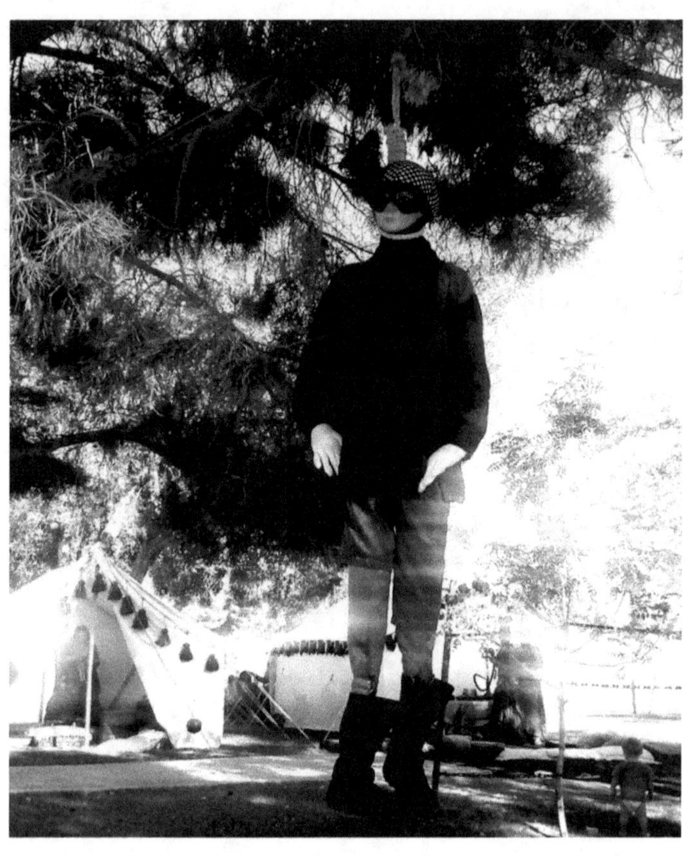

In every era, the Harlequin-Fool is made an Example of by the Fear-Adoring All-Categorizing, Perpetually-Commenting Congress of Tepid Force that takes the Wilds out of our Hearts, replacing them with Tics, Fears and Pettiness. But the Forest King perseveres in her mayhems, even when she is caught, even while her woods are burned down.

REMAIN A FOOL-KING

JOIN THE IRON GARTERS

THE IRON GARTERS AND THEIR MANY MASKS

AN INCONCLUSIVE HISTORY

Our immediate progenitors, those fellow sorcerers Deleuze and Guattari, said, "The earth needs a new romanticism." They were perhaps echoing Novalis, the Night poet, who once exclaimed, "The world must be romanticized. This yields again its original meaning. Romanticizing is nothing else than a qualitative potentization... By giving the common a higher meaning, the everyday a mysterious semblance, the known the dignity of the unknown, the finite the appearance of the infinite, I romanticize it...." Then, much later, in a different context, *The Cramps'* singer Lux Interior said, "Let's Tear This Damn Place Up," wearing nothing but torn lingerie and his own blood.

It would be easy for some to conclude: Idiots, Maniacs, Naïfs. It would be easy to assume the political and the social is nowhere operative.

But first, a Garter would ask: which version of idiocy or mania or *naïveté* do you refer? Perhaps it's that fanged invisibility that creaks the meadows and turns the woods to vibrating onyx? Or the lunar frisson that coaxes the tides into spumes of amber, anointing a sex-and-food drenched

PROTO-BULLETIN · SOMA, SAN FRANCISCO, SPRING 2004

afternoon? Or is it that breath of beyond—some remembered passage in a fantasy paperback, or a funereal spice from a vagrant witch—that runs untrammeled through the metropolis to lure the wayfarer down heaths and moors into *hinterlands*? The world is strewn with real souls, emitting; a world as such is the ever-shifting totality of souls in various frequencies of expression. We aren't saying we are essentially romantic but we are saying that our perspectives and speculations are *very* functional: they yield means and results, oblique pathways and open spaces, refreshing vantages and tactical beachheads. Perceptual play declaims new territories in space-time that accommodates more energies and more lives. So again, we are at the very burning heart of the political and the social: *spaciousness* and how to vivify it, perpetuate it and perfect it, especially when the walls are closing in and the mind and heart are threatened with reduction.

The earth needs new *un-knowings* that are revelatory and healing and space-making. It's high time to surrender our credibilities, our neuroses, our identity-fixes when the darkness is most opaque, while also the most voluble; but then in the hot pit of darkness, to reassert our reverential, battle-born enthusiasms when the very conditions for life are threatened. The earth needs new errant dialogues and speculative tangents that wander and spasm across barriers and categories without the fascistic tic to quickly reestablish and reassert the faux-authority of those troubled boundaries. The earth needs new sensualities that derive from the energies released when borders are crossed and unlegislated desires are smuggled, or simply when particularities, like stones and glass shards, are allowed to breathe and blossom inside the Present.

The Garters are saboteurs, smugglers, cultural engineers, phantasy tacticians, living out, in the words of poet

Hart Crane, an "improved infancy." They materialize wherever art and education realign as one border-crossing provocation. For in the worlds that matter to us and which we strive to recreate, creativity and pedagogy were never sundered, art and politics were never at each other's throats, but one was forever inextricably in love with the other. So in the dominant prejudices of early twenty-first century America, the Garters by default are called *criminals*—which certainly expands our repertoire, improves our wardrobes and enriches our sex lives. We are called *criminals* because we are ineluctably *judged* and yet we strive *always* to elude judgment. However, Judgment is never wholly eluded but then we are never wholly judged either. All judgment is predicated on economic logic these days; whatever saves us from risk, expenditure, inconvenience, attentiveness is deemed the preferred currency. So it is our vital imperative to create and unleash new predicates that *look* and act like *crimes*, i.e. *invitations to strangeness.* Lastly: performing as criminals, and assuming the personae of the outlaw exacerbates our available energies, feeds our libidinal reservoirs and creates auras of the sublime about us that many people have forgotten that they can experience. And thus we serve the social, even as we un-serve it.

So what are the criminal masks these Garters wear?

In one of their desert mobilizations, the Iron Garters is a syndicate that meets in Las Vegas to discuss and ponder and plot desire, sexuality, taboos, Eros and the body through the medium of writing and propaganda. What flees through sensation we attempt to transcribe in syllables. What distorts the subtleties of its own collisions we awkwardly harvest. Above all we revere the infinity of the sexual in the very midst of our aroused conversing. We share books, visions, tales, jokes, movies, songs and examples that drive, trouble, tantalize and excite us. We have "conversations" that are entirely unresolvable and thus fecund, not beholden to one form of certainty, opinion or stance. Garters believe that conversations, instead of positions, attitudes, conclusions, and credentials are far more conducive to radical deviations and flowerings of culture.

In another, coastal version the Garters are a theory and politics obsessed art group from the Oakland/San Francisco area who engage in transformative social practices and semi-illegal infiltrations. Writing is also heavily involved, as is gardening, vaudeville, rabblerousing, open schools, wanderings, magic and street lectures. Above all, this mutation of the Iron Garters is overly concerned with how economic monocultures have voided urban spaces of their emancipatory and healing potentials. Where politics has failed, art rushes in with all its reparative powers at full burn. This version of the Garters is going through a catalytic transformation and taking on more pedagological imperatives.

But then also, in Nether-where, the Garters exist as the semi-fictional, quasi-imaginary protectors and smugglers of a fragile virus-borne ecosystem called *Noctula* whose *transmedial* expressions are currently being documented and archived by the current author. This version of the Garters believes sincerely that the Human and the *Anthropocene* need a bracing dose of the Alien to refine our individual consciousness and to reform and reimagine habitable realities. Herein is where magick, speculative philosophy, magical realism, slime science all dissolve and hybridize into one mad devotional Weltanschauung. Here seethes realms of theory-fiction, philosophy-theater, poetic-supernaturalism, gnostic contagions, Artaudian becomings, and Deleuzian sorceries. This Garter world is organized through a volatile and dynamic eroticism that encompasses much more than just sexual and romantic love.

We believe that a Movement or Force, a Revolutionary Vanguard or Radical Mobilization, for it to persist more dynamically and with sustained furor against overwhelming odds, its own internal contradictions, ceaselessly cruel oppressors, or just the "normal" fluctuations of being, must articulate and sustain itself on multiple yet simultaneously fused levels. In a word: militant versatility. Is it any wonder that poor Guy Debord became so obsessed with military strategizing? Anything remotely called a counter-culture must consider and plan its own defenses and maneuverings against invalidation, consolidation, irrelevancy and destruction. *War-machine*, D&G called it—and I don't think we've even begun to consider the ramifications of this concept for art and culture, social practice and radical becoming.

So the fictional-poetic-mythic escapades of the Iron Garters in their magical, Atlantean ecosphere of *Noctula,* as a *transmedial* venture of the poetic imagination serves as a reservoir for *real* energy, tactics, inspiration, intensities to be mined and immediately used in "Real Life," especially when the less-fictional escapades and energies of so-called "real life" Garters becomes spent or frazzled or derailed. This is the Guerrilla *'pataphysical* approach to reality: one must always elaborate, populate, nourish and sustain counter-worlds, counter-alibis, counter-selves, counter-myths that are not necessarily "real," and that can be plugged into, inhabited, invoked, evoked, shared and released in the real world, not only for their reparative, nourishing powers but for the *complex* and *necessary* demands they make on your and other's status quos/reality versions. Always, minute-by-minute, the wear and tear of existence catches up, our fantasies and dreams in perpetual fragmentation, our hopes and loves threatened by invalidation, our anxieties and fears gurgling up from the collective howl, so re-fortifying ourselves through the malleable, indestructible ether of the Imaginary is a necessary political tool.

This proposal also releases a question into the normalization of games in daily consumer life. Which counter-worlds are *actually* benefiting us, helping us to "flourish"—in the term used by social theorist Lauren Berlant.

The Iron Garters have become, by necessity, this simultaneity of forms, alliances, methods, logics and mythologies. What unifies them in their various documented and undocumented forms is the passionate and voracious necessity to trouble and often brashly dissolve the ideological barriers separating crime from community, religion from science, philosophy from spirituality, the occult from the rational, the school from the streets, work from play, the sacred from the profane, the exalted from the banal, the empirical from the speculative, and the ugly from the beautiful. They suggest an invitation to an Outside that also requires novel and more attentive cultivations of the Interior. This is border *work,* which, by necessity is dangerous and ambiguous, involving taboo-splicing, contraband-disrobing, uncanny-infiltrating among our many indispensable crafts. We are especially interested in how Theory can overflow and outgrow its comfortable habituations/assumptions and reassert its artful, playful influences on various reality modes. The very "otherances" Theory gives such lip service to become rapidly tamed/defanged by the dominant institutions that depend on Theory's "inoculated" reproducibilities in the first place. We believe in brutal critiques of existing institutions insofar as such critiques provoke the creations of new institutions, articulations, accommodations. But we also need approachable, workable examples and actual contexts to set our rhetoric lose within. We can't just keep it in expensive books sitting inside imposing buildings. We are here to build in space/time, with flesh and with breath, with labyrinths and with fields.

(What is an institution? A gang is one type, freighted with the panic-driven and libidinal-manias that are usually sanctioned only by "nature." The police are another institution that garners similar affects as a gang. Both institutions would be served by a deep and irresponsible Erotic makeover.)

Radical change—or, in Deleuze's words, "a moment of shattering unity"—won't happen just in schools, knitting circles, community gardens, publishing houses, or largely white, heterosexual anarchist collectives, although those are all provocative sites for Garters to hone their tactics, critiques, experiments and subversions. But Transformations *will* happen in overlapping, interwoven and infiltrated/infiltrating milieus of all sorts, especially the *surprising* and *oft-forgotten/overlooked* ones. These hybrid sites are where conversations of word and act take place between different entities, and experiments both rational and feral are collectively and singularly undertaken. All the while, participants retain and nourish *feelings* of excitement and intensity that the more "professional" and "hierarchical' institutions, the ones rigidly hierarchized, traditionally bankrolled and officially named, tend to suppress, mock and sublimate.

So pick a place that has no legible name or clear protocol. Perhaps this place is in your very home or office. These places are often the most neglected or taken-for-granted zones or milieus in our daily blind habitualness. The corner of the white picket fence, the utility walkway, the median strip, the blank field, the vacant lot, the soulless desk. Then momentarily, contextually, *define* this place by the verbs it induces, the nouns it uncovers, the syntaxes it secretes: politics as art, space as syntax, affect as locus.

END BULLETIN

MANIFESTO FOR YES/TRES/PASS/INC!

BY M. BALTHAZAR B. DE COVERLY.

Instead of decrying the death of youth, counterculture, innovation, freedom, and happiness, it is instead in my best interest to do something I should have done every time I wanted to do something: trespass. Trespassing is not anything original or inherently revolutionary: civilization, itself, is based on many forms of political, economic and martial trespassing of some sort. Despite the seemingly criminal nature of such an act, it is rather perfectly respectful of the infinitude of boundaries, segments, borders and lines that demarcate our wide, wild world. By deeming it exciting, liberating and orgasmic to trespass, the trespasser is not only granting himself or herself full sovereignty but also bestowing importance on whatever line was trespassed in the process. When we say Yes Trespassing! We are using an old ruse: putting opposites where they don't belong, thus using simplicity to confound the masses. When we do Trespass and don't get caught, the orgasm of secrecy is our gift and no one's the wiser.

Trespassing marks the profound moment where the individual can express his deepest desires within a context that would normally reject them, with or without the knowledge of said context. Most often this forced incubation of desire within an "official" or "professional" vesSel is the closest any one of us will get to tasting the Promethean freedom hinted at by any number of [illegible] Anarchists, Monarchists and Radical Militiamen. Instead of the impossible rhetoric of the Trust Fund Black Blockers that reeks of empty gesturalism, we would supplant such tidy double negatives, with direct action that confounds all manner of public and private, sacred and profane, not as a way to blaspheme per se, but to excite; not to merely disrespect but to adjust particular homages; not as a way to dilly-dally in adolescent marketable rebellion but to refocus the lens of revolt; not as a way to steal from Big Brother but to demonstrate the numerous Little Big Brothers that are far easier to rob from.

In most situations, purpose, incentive, and motivation are ready-made and built into whatever context you find yourself in. Thus, by being opposed to spontaneity, they are corrossive. When you find yourself in traffic, nothing is more annoying because your purpose there is so obvious: to get out of traffic to whatever destination you had in mind before you got in. Built-in algebras of purpose, incentive, and motivations are obvious in the workplace, the marketplace, the beverageplace; each social context comes with its own readymades that everyone is more than willing to take for granted figuring they have no other choice. But within the dense shell of Officility and Professionally-meted out Purpose, lurks real life, as nonchalent as a pillow fight in a canning factory, but as vicious as a botanist shooting heroin with a Bird of Paradise. Just as the Official Contexts have their own vertiginious labyrinths and paper trails of documentation, red tape, permits, prohibitions, taxations and certifications, so Desire forms its own offensive paper trails, mocking and trespassing the Official; these paper trails will be accumulated from all over the world as Evidence of Real Life; such actions can be in the way of performance, plagiarism, music, live fucking, eavesdropping, detective work, embezzlement, and art.

TRESPASSIONS UNLIMITED [illegible]

This is a very early version of the Iron Garters, known as *Trespassions Unlimited*, or *Yes/Tres/Pass/Inc* and their first written manifesto distributed in SoMa, San Francisco.

THE EARLIEST "OFFICIAL" BULLETIN

Welcome, *Mature* Pleasure Seeker!

The Iron Garters is a radical street gang that accepts everybody provided they show *mettle* and *leg*. We spice our utterances with a vocabulary fermented in the gutters and the libraries, as well as the fields and alleys that rise and fall sloppily between. Most of what we've learned about terminology happened in a euphoric tour through the corner drugstore. There is wildness we want to possess us but also new domesticities we want to warm our grimy toes. We pan our hungers between forests and hearths, knowing that wastelands outnumber us, but that they are treasure-seeded for the cunning.

Yes, we are verbose, yes, we are clumsy, yes, we are no-brow; are we also Methodical? Elegant? Versatile? Cryptic? Given that we are those other things, then yes we are these things too, so much so that the strengths of Negation we wield are many-pronged, dizzying and incarnational. Our "No" infiltrates the manufactured skins of things, and implants a "YES," wildly ambiguous in its tentacle resonances, rising to the surface to alchemize the cracks and flecks into far more radiant flecks and cracks. This is the alchemy by which we fuck the given, no matter how it terminally chastises us.

Why Iron Garters, the Name?

We are *ostranenie* but also *unheimlich*. The Garter is snake and leash; fang and lash; a bind and a vow; a double-edged tongue of attack and retreat; submission and domination; the play of oppositions in all their entangling, energizing contradictions. Garter is a Sign of the thigh's upward plunge into rapturous intimacy; as well as the toe's downward reach into primal loam; it is the insignia of an Event that is potentially climactic or catastrophic but which cannot be limited in its expressiveness or open-endedness. Many of us have seen how the sensorial, polyglot play of metal and fabric, glass and bone can make us feel more empowered; fashion is always about forces more violently archaic than what is just fashionable. We are celebrators and instigators of every erotic and insurrectionary outburst but we pull it all off with hypnotic style, conspiratorial complicity and inclusive nonchalance. Iron is a recognizable term for resilience that can be eroticized. Subtlety is an ironclad force that seduces with painstaking vigor. Even though the world is over-determined by forces we have no control over, Garters secrete *territory* for delight and play wherever they throng, from the most denuded office space to the most unencumbered prairie. They don't need "special" spaces to pull off special deeds, although a clubhouse, especially if its flimsy, scary-looking and hard to access is a good place to congregate and roughhouse. When you think of the gentle sting of a garter belt you don't think of iron chains or serpent's fangs. For the Garters, what isn't necessarily thought at first is what we compel at first. Since all living is relating, and all relating is performing, we will perform and smuggle the most ingenious relations.

We are not interested in new members unless they can reconcile the most gregarious and generous topologies inside themselves. They have to exercise on a constant basis a radical imagination that is, above all participatory and versatile. The spaces within determine the spaces without; and vice versa. For instance, if our interior psychic spaces feel beset by an always-reverberating Command to Justify, Resemble, Defend, Legitimize then we must let the Wild Outside flood us for purification and readjustment. Your leg is both your leg, and something more scintillating and cryptic, that collides with and divides up space into qualitative moments. Mettle is many things too, all of which may be seductive, depending on how far you want to take it, and how generous you are in the taking. There is sovereignty in vulnerability, just as there is sex in trash. The stars render us defenseless in our representations, so always defer to the Outside.

How and why does one become a Garter?

Becoming a Garter means becoming who you already want to be. It means entering into your own oceanic reverberations and being swept away by them. We are not presuming to know *what* you want to be, only that you, indeed, *want to be.* And at every moment too, this kernel of need and crisis cries out to you to be honored and embodied and deployed in different ways. Thus, Garter is a placeholder name for the oft-secretive, always-dynamic, habitually-suppressed flux of fantasies, hunches, excitations, riddles, lusts, fixations, errors, minutiae, inklings, reveries, cartographies, red herrings, personae, obsessions and absurdities inside of you (yet always in inextricable overlap with the world's chorus) that make life more wonderful and empowering when they can be accessed, exercised, played with, worked with and released.

The Earth likes your dreams, especially when they involve Her. Fictions are real, insofar as they inject truth-potentials into your living. Sometimes it takes conspiratorial and clandestine energies to release them, however: the tribal braggadocio of a secret society, an outlaw gang, a governmental agency, or a Masonic lodge. All who use exclusion and opacity to consolidate isolating and hierarchical power will be likewise used and manipulated by us to disseminate and release *other* kinds of power. It is not our privilege to tell your what this *other* means.

The process of Gartering is rigorous, intricate, bewildering, alter-sensical and requiring several hair-raising initiations. A first tenet for potential initiates: American society, or whatever that has come to mean, has dissolved any interest in the initiatory, replacing it instead, with the deformational. So instead of seizing the immediacy of experiences, we immediately suffer the seizing away of our experiences. Nothing we experience matters unless it has cash value in someone else's eyes. But take away the cash, you still have matter being itself, becoming it/other selves, *mattering*, vibrating in heat and energy inside a similarly resonating cosmos. That's an open secret we can share right now.

Thus, prospective Garter, your initiations will be many, depending upon the energies and excitements you bring to bear upon them. The prospective member should consider the following alliances the Garters have made: Spiritually, Garters are aligned with Sophia (Wisdom/Knowledge) and her holy consort, the Cosmic Hermaphrodite and their plethora of metamorphoses and passages. This is intricate *theopolitical* and *theopoetic* territory that will piecemeal, tantalizingly be conveyed to initiates through word, gesture, embrace, encounter and fire. But Garters are radical pluralists and encourage you to weave together your own cosmologies and theogonies based, at least, on the idea that the Cosmos is a living playground of *daemonic* and erotic and relational potentials. Moreover, there are many among us who know that the divisions between philosophy and religion, poetry and mysticism, pragmatism and sorcery, theory and poetry—or however the muck you want to distinguish these things—need to be dissolved. This will be explored in a more in-depth communiqué at some indefinite juncture.

Socially, Garters are reviving the weapons that Dada and Punk and the Situationists and all those ’60s street gangs harnessed. But even so, we will reference other groups, some quite forgotten, like the Suicide Club and the International Necronautical Society, while making strikingly tangential cross-hatchings. We will also show how most of these groups fell quite short of their own desires and visions. For instance, the Situationists lacked class consciousness, intersectionality, economics and feminism, among other elephants in the room. Dada was meant to implode and not endure; even its implosion was a betrayal of Dada. Many ’60s gangs reasserted tediously oppressive gender roles that kept women under boot and heel. “Anarchist thinkers”—whose vocabularies can be as enchanting as the Rhineland Mystics—Hakim Bey, Jack Black, and *CrimethInc.* all too often espouse a shopping mall, juvenile individualism that overlooks This Fact that for many of us:

Our labors and our games are not in opposition, they are in harmonic syzygy. Secondly, we are not afraid to toil for the sake of *more* euphoric energy. Thirdly, often the most supreme idleness or exquisite languor is unified within our most complex and arduous projects.

Finally, contemporary "adventure groups," while they love to intellectualize their own *trespassions*, often recoil before theories, voices, testaments, and daily barbarities that don't reinforce their own *Übermensch* impressiveness. We offer these all-too-brief critiques as kindling for active thought, and as fodder for vitriolic critique of us. For without critique, we cannot create, and vice versa. We are *sensitive*, yes, but sensitivity works only if it is flush with change, which is the blood of creativity.

Speaking of Kulchur—the Garters know that the Eye & Value, when wedded, defangs and tames almost any cultural explosion/expression turning it into once-and-future trash. But in place of an ironic acquiescence to market forces, we suggest the playground tactics of the saboteur and the smuggler: using evasion, disguise, cryptologies, misleading mythologies, we will "hide" what is most sacred to us, while giving away, to be re-appropriated, the mere baubles of our ecstasies. Every Garter shall learn how to build their own Sanctuaries that are always being smuggled through enemy lines. This is one of the secrets of secrecy: we all need it to perpetuate the healing fictions of our lives.

Style-wise, Garters play with, mutate, exploit and subvert the iconographies and idolatries of biker gangs, corsairs, street hustlers, punk rockers, sailors, fetishists, witches, runaways, autodidacts, sadomasochists, anarchists, pill-poppers, junkyard preachers and pansexuals.

Politically, we adore and strive for Kropotkin's Mutual Aid, in its many paradoxical flowerings, as well as the potentials of igniting catalytic play among care-giving individuals distributed in large or small or unquantifiable groups.

Play = Labor
Style = Vision
Desire = Alliance
Context = Energy

These are four formulae that Garters employ in their daily encounters with entities and things and which form the synthesis of their Political Vision(s). When one term can so easily be seen to live in and be charged by the other, than a moment reconfigures into more generous, labyrinthine appearances. Whatever dreams we suppress for decorum's sake are worn loud yet bafflingly on our vests, dresses, capes, negligees, corsages. We all want to be part of a secret tribe, especially if it encourages us to get primordial with *Others*. There is a secret to secrecy that more obtuse thinkers like Lacan and Derrida were quite aware of, but couldn't quite make sexy; however, it takes a real gang, such as ours, and who often assume a confusingly religious mantle, to put that secrecy into action. The affective results of using secrecy for empowerment, excitations, and mobilization? A wildness is released through implications, emitted, secreted and that is strangely coherent and organizational the more it touches and plays with things. Garters will make you wilder (you will have no choice) and thus: more joyous, more capable, more generous. Illusion is a Revolutionary Weapon! to quote our friends, the INS.

We use political terms how radical Spinozists would: joy as the capacity for more constructive, euphoric activity, complex relations and creative entanglements. Capability as a more nuanced and accommodating perception that eases into chaos like heated lingerie. Generosity as a way of communicating with and among Others, while also enlivening their modes of being, especially when the possibilities of communication and enlivening seem most direly impossible. Garters are instinctual gift-givers, stemming from the fact that their very existence is a gift to a fear-poisoned, uninspired society.

Explain again what it means to show mettle and leg? Answer: Potentials for endless *synecdoche.* As Garters we look to the endless arsenal of Greek Rhetoric for terms that can beneficially contort our actions and ideas. "Leg" can mean anything you choose to reveal and "mettle" can mean anything you choose to flex. For Garters, revelation requires well-plotted, exquisite subtlety and methodical seductions. As much as sex sells, insinuation and intrigue last longer and are more durable, more mobile. Garters engage in a complicated and showy mating dance with life, involving displays of erotic heraldry, artistic tributes and hermetic ready-mades. All Garters are erotic, even if they are asexual, for desire is a mobile homeland animated by Primordial Love and Visceral Devotion. The Garters embrace a polymorphous, pansexual, ever-shifting, biocentric, ever-queering conception of Eros, sexuality and desire. That should set your imagination reeling, so surrender, with cunning to the maelstrom of your own passions.

In militantly organizing like a masonic-type secret society, and mobilizing like an outlaw biker gang, we will unleash our group desires in ways that are radically different from the exhausted routines and protocols of restaurant, bar, car, private residence, text message, tweet, Facebook, bedroom, sex, sleep, anxiety dreams. Becoming socialized means we've been coerced to reveal things we didn't want to and flex other things that hurt us. Becoming socialized to the entrenched hierarchies means we must now engage in healing acts that come from orchestrated mayhem and estranging choreographies. The Iron Garters never forget that "man" is the "rationalizing animal"; the Garters, true to form, are also animals, rationalizing alienated forms of reason and forgotten acts of healing.

The Garter doesn't want to be buried with the phrase, "S/he played it safe" indelibly written on their tomb. Nor do Garters deliberately and destructively seek danger. Self-destruction *is* the status quo. What Garters court are the oblique byways of Uncertainty and the Unknown; and the ingenuity of their courtship rites creates a durable craft upon which to navigate. Ritual and devotion, play and collaboration are the planks and nails that keep the craft afloat. Garters never forget that what is at stake is what is Ventured. Our bodies and minds have ossified into positions and attitudes we never desired. The most dominant and thus most ossified Social Organizations that rely on profit, repetition, subservience, and inner and outer warmongering conveniently forget that they are destroying us. The Iron Garters will rectify this forgetfulness by forcing other ways of organizing space and the organisms that play in it. Gangs can do this with ease because wherever they move they bring transformative ravishment, lively confusion, contagious mystery and genuine Panic. In assuming the scuzzy raiments of what tactful, prestige-driven society fears most, we are guaranteeing that the passersby who deplore us the most shall have the most memorable night.

In truth, the Iron Garters are smugglers of a magical ecosystem that can manifest and be secreted anywhere, given the correct correspondences. This is the counter-world fiction that supplements our day-light, real-world ventures. We have a tendency to suggest that these correspondences, when emitted in the "real world" conspire to create feelings, affects, occasions, and events that we call Sacred—a force that tends to undo the artificial restrictions that humans, in their ideologically-driven fears, have imposed upon reality. Rites of theater, ritual, picnic, pilgrimage, rides, raids, expeditions, dog-piles, mud fights, mystical declarations: these are ways of creating new physical, geographical, erotic, spiritual and emotional territories. By masquerading as archetypal "criminals" we are living reminders of the porousness of categories and the desperate need for societies to reinvent themselves thru the radical imagination.

END BULLETIN

A GARTER LOVE LETTER LOST IN THE SHUFFLE

We will not feel judged to the point of inaction, to the point of panic. Panic is there intact, flush with the earth. It grows in the trees and the mortar we build our offices with. Judgment, as a form only achieves stasis, not transformation.

We need Messengers instead of Judges.
Movements instead of paralyses.
"Eroticizing problems as games" : propositions that move.

Let us hearken to this inner counsel, however questionable, with its outer noise, figments/fragments, loud trash, sifted and reworked; we need to listen to what the world asks because these questions are the world, so they reverberate within us. This mosaic is choral.

These questions don't depart; posing them, they become the very problems that invite you into the Dance. I was blessed to even be hearing such questions addressed to me in the first place, especially in the company of friends who have their own ways of entering into these questions.

How comforting to not be judged, but to sit at exhilarating ease, as if in an overflowing banquet before a fatal contest, amid such insistent questions –

The bravery of my friends is astonishing.

The braver our companions, the more our questions are workable and relatable. You need exemplary lovers and allies, platonic and erotic, both/and, otherwise, reinventing camaraderie, love. Around now, our early to mid [illegible], questions grow more jagged and more insistent, as they come with events that test our endurance, our speech, and our work.

"Shame is also a force wielded by consensus marketplace reality to manufacture servile, unmotivated, identity-dependent, and "de-souled" individuals. Shame is a way to de-wild the human being and to eradicate any aspects that seem atavistic, feral, creative, or irrational."

—BURDINA GALTZARI operative
(which is a translation of Iron Garter)

SAN FRANCISCO, SUMMER 2012

OUR STRANGE ATTRACTORS

ON *POETICS*, OR WORLD-MAKING

Propositions to immediately put into action:

1. My capacity for doing good is directly related to my capacity for wonder. If I'm not awed, how can I care? Why should I? In place of oppressively dogmatic religions, ethically void politics, soul-bankrupt infotainments, and atheist-humanist solipsisms: a mature, proactive and extremely bold enchantment with this world, engendering versatile ethics, perpetuating labyrinthine engagements, promoting a "tough" romanticism that is neither naïve, simplistic, selfish or vulgar. Emotions are not commentaries; sensations are not positions. But both are ways, fluid and shifting into manifold Others.

2. In place of the language of advertisement, connivance, debate, minutiae fatigue, compulsive salesmanship, nefarious abridgement, convenient reductionism, addictive meme-ing and kneejerk oneupmanship: a subtle, nuanced, lyrical foray in many clashing voices that insists on *defamiliarizing* what is taken for granted, of taking the *strange* for

the ground that we work with, then working/playing with the intimacies hidden in our own estrangements. We want to reawaken the clashing songs inside of every word, so our bodies will have things radiant to throw forth as gifts and lures.

3. "You have to be enamored of the world," Jane Bennett explains, in order to contribute your "scarce mortal services" to others (Jane Bennett, *The Enchantment of Modern Life*). We are not afraid of affection, romance, devotion, cathexis, entanglement, charity, fixation, expenditure and obsession, for we know they are but processes among processes, fleeting yet vivifying passages we explore with the heartiest possible torches; in turn they bring us into newer, more elaborate passages, or even, newer, duller passages.

4. The inherent ordeal is how to preserve enchantment in spite of the pricks and snares and shit-falls of what's Real. It's what you do with Disappointment and Derailment, through language, through telling, through activity, through sound, through movement that demarcates the bounds of your integrity. Were there a war of the Soul it would consist in inflicting transformation on states of being that seem insupportable and intransigent; of making, through cultivated artistry and visionary ritual, *being* predicated on *becoming*, while also, paradoxically knowing that such becoming must be experienced by a real, fully-fleshed someone.

5. Realism, when it is enriched and edified by meticulous poetic language, becomes ennobling and visionary, and not just caustic and hard-boiled and cynical (in the latter-day definition of the word.) We must hone an uncanny ear for things that "speak for themselves," which is *matter matter-*

ing[1], and not relinquishing singularity to ideas and ideals. Ideas work insofar as they tend to induce energies.

6. Realism *is* perceptual vertigo, the *arch* poetic struggle, in which our limited sensual apparatuses must allow and encourage passage for extra-sensual, extra-human vectors. We must become radios, terminals, nexuses, way-stations, transmitters and portals for forces and agents we hardly have words for. If we make maps of these presences, we might be able to inhabit the moments with a fuller sense of companionship.

7. To *not* let "things speak for themselves" is the betrayal endemic to bad poetics, bad ethics, bad writing, and bad speech and becomes more generally the foreclosure of anything political or ethical. However, a single voice, as we shall see, is always choral.

8. We are never giving our voices to things, but letting things overlay our own voices with theirs. In the process—which is all we are anyway—a choral mosaic is woven and maintained: something *kosmic* is kept at a high pitch.

9. No despair but clarity, even when shipwrecked in a blood gutter. This clarity is a political commitment to things *thinging*. We will hear what is said, we will let the voices interfere with us, even from the mutest, the dingiest and the most *gutterized*. We will be attentive to the paltriest stammerings, for they are integral to the structure, which, itself, is structureless when scrutinized.

1 We borrow this lovely and evocative term from a kindred art group called the INS, or the International Necronautical Society. *The Mattering of Matter* is their own collection of bulletins and manifestos, which we passionately recommend.

10. We think warmly of Michael McClure's "structureless structure"; we know that chaos is not disorder but a dazzling complexity that requires the playful labors of finely-tuned, subtle, empathetic and voracious perceptions; we hearken to the roots of the word subtlety: "finely-woven." We aspire for an intimacy with things that straddles both chaos and order and the subtle in-mixings of both.

11. We only speak (and thus, be) through intricate relationality: William James beautifully asserts: "Every definite image in the mind is steeped and dyed in the free water that flows round it. With it goes the sense of its relations, near and remote."

12. Words mean things and should be honored, not cheapened, not monumentalized; but also their honor is dependent on the river they are in. We are cultivators of the river, which is to say, of what the river is, which is many and one, swift yet sluggish, veering yet dead-on.

13. When Lyn Hejinian writes about Gertrude Stein, she makes a critical distinction between "entity" and "identity" in the compositional work that Stein pursues (Hejinian, "Three Lives"). Entity is the astonishment of being anything at all it hardly matters what and identity is the shock of composing oneself in time and seeing revisions accumulate on you *as* you.

14. Both entity and identity are modes of attention that overlap and feed into and with each other in creativity. They allow for survival as well as adventure; keeping these in relative harmonies is perpetuated by the fineness and subtlety of our visionary ear, our ability to hearken to ourselves and others.

15. We grow accustomed to the non-human and welcome its incursions. We know that the human as hub of creation is, at best, a false alarm. But as humans, and more specifically as artists, we must attempt to render these non-human invasions that beset us with the language available, no matter how paltry and insufficient it seems. If this means changing the language to better hear the salvos from the Unknown, we must be prepared. If it means importing or deriving new symbols from archaic vocabularies, we must lend the generous ear.

16. Thus we depart from Mina Loy's own gorgeous *ars poetica*: "I must live in my lantern/Trimming subliminal flicker/Virginal to the bellows/Of Experience" (Loy, 53).

17. From Derrida, we learn that writing's detours, deflections and displacements are but alternate messengers crying out to us in clashing voices. Having no choice but to hear, we have no choice but to be changed—and to embrace these rigorous transmutations.

18. We believe in *being* that cries out to be altered, *identity* that begs to be divested of its jewels, and *life* that is hungry for other lives to overtake it.

19. Serial metamorphosis = ontological versatility.

20. Seers of *otherances* naturally have more intriguing things to say.

21. Surprise, the secret.

22. "To think is not to get out of the cave; it is not to replace the uncertainty of shadows by the clear-cut outlines of

things themselves, the flame's flickering glow by the light of the true sun. To think is to enter the Labyrinth; more exactly, it is to make be and appear a Labyrinth when we might have stayed 'lying among the flowers, facing the sky.' It is to lose oneself amidst galleries which exist only because we never tire of digging them; to turn round and round at the end of a cul-de-sac whose entrance has been shut off behind us—until, inexplicably, this spinning round opens up in the surrounding walls cracks which offer passage"

—Cornelius Castoriadis

23. The cultivation of the labyrinth, however is not caffeinated haphazardry, businessman's chicanery, nihilistic chaos, burning man self-indulgence; but a deliberation (in the Thoreauvian sense) in which improvisation and venture, derailment and determination, failure and flailing—the very strata of our characters—all work together as long as we are sincerely absorbed by the work so much so that it *becomes* play.

Often the most meaningless of templates, i.e. existence offers the most potentials for rapturous tapestries.

24. The work is the secret. It is open for us to live through, a passage of passages.

END BULLETIN

PRELIMINARY NOTES ON LOVE AND EROS

Strangeness, unnamed and unchecked intercedes in our lives. Sometime it is a global event with hauntingly local effects. It comes highly concentrated in other people. Certain strangeness enchants, while other kinds wound; yet still others are neutral and "ontologically indescribable." Often the repercussions of a strange event or a strange person aren't felt until after the event, in laughs, sobs, shudders and flails. A car accident, an altercation with a "crazy" person, a moment of unexpected violence, or a feeling of "offness" inside the body are all strange events we've experienced. They are disruptive if you become overly entangled in their energies or are blithely inattentive to their ramifications. With strangeness you must walk that fine line: *vigilant insouciance*. And the strangeness that is, arguably the most entangling is the romantic and erotic kind.

In every epoch certain courageous explorers rediscover the primacy of Love, as both the primordial force of Eros and as the only pragmatic path towards individual and collective redemption. Yet every epoch seems to forget or forgo this epiphany. Rather, it cannot be distributed in such unquantifiable doses. The Garters would say the reason is, as it has always been: Fear. But the only Fear that exists is the fear of destruction, of losing one's identity or meanings in something larger, nameless, more unfathomable. We cling desperately to whatever affiliation, credential, trophy or reminder keeps us seemingly grounded, while Eros keeps cajoling us off every cliff we see. So we fear Love. And in fearing it, we fear and eschew Life.

When this Fear eclipses the Self or the Social, then Eros and Love, once more, become either naïve myths or foolhardy commitments that only fools or mystics undertake. They are no longer seen as primordial energies that can transform our terrestrial conditions, as well as the subjectivities that spatter the earth. Likewise, they are no longer seen as the *prima materia* of radically participatory philosophical engagement.

Love's range is boundless, as Hesiod knew when he granted prestige to the "Cosmogonic Eros" as the generative force of creation. This Eros, of course, exceeds any straightforward, rational or convenient ideas we might have about it, which might be why its potential healing powers are often forsaken or neglected. For Eros implies a certain relation with Chaos that seems inconvenient and frightening but is also exemplified by the world as it is, in the process of its perpetual fluctuations, vivid errancies, and entropic spasms. My own conceptions of healing, before I became a Garter, conflated it with "judgment" of my own being; a judgment implying that I was "broken" and needed to be fixed, that my maladies were an incriminatory difference to be smoothed over and normalized, rectified into some abnormally static equilibrium. But in fact, brokenness is the given, and, indeed, already a holism, so healing instead is simply care for the parts that is constant and love-driven.

Equilibrium is but a moment of balance among energizing imbalances.

Poets and artists like Walt Whitman and Austin Spare have hinted at such a Cosmic Eros. Thinkers like Ludwig Klages have been quite explicit about its power. More contemporary philosophers like Gilles Deleuze, bell hooks, and Alain Badiou have explored in depth new ways of thinking about love, Eros and desire that entail a more *cosmic* outlook. Hugely integral to this cosmic view is that Love doesn't require a Thing to have, hold, lack or pine for. Rather, Love is the movement that renders the world alive and buzzing with relational energy.

It was in the desert that I came upon a notion of Eros as a way of working, practically and spiritually with Chaos and with the volatile energies that it entails. This suggests a form of Love that is *ecological* in its thinking, which is to say, a Love that considers the myriad relations and inter-workings between entities and energies on all planes of existence. If I think of the spiritual labor that humans will have to take upon themselves if they want to endure, it can only be in terms of *ecology*: of how to harmonize the myriad, animated parts that are flush with a world, of how to live richly among scarcities, of how to sacrifice small gratifications for larger ecstasies, and of how to navigate new and unusual sensations among unusually divergent entities.

Love as the ecological force par excellence is a complex assertion that the Garters are bringing forth into the gutters of this young century. Such a love is, of course, "hard work," necessitating risk, failure, collapse and blindness, among other pitfalls, but also insuring potential union with "others" in ways that conventional ideas of love may not encourage. This more cosmic love stands in direct relation to an unknown, which is both fearful and catalyzing. It also interrogates the possessiveness, materialism and codependence—in a word, the fear—rampant in certain ideas of romantic love.

The doctrine, especially in Western culture, of "love" as a tortured search for idealized, mythic completion through another person, thing, or idea must be ruthlessly questioned and thereby lovingly subverted. This isn't to say that love should *not* be entered into passionately and madly—for indeed, the tensions induced by the passions are inherently creative and thus supremely Erotic in their manifestations. The discerning psyche, however, or the Gartered Soul must be able to pass through such passions, such obsessions without being destroyed or nullified by them. To turn the injurious into the edifying is what magic is. Nobody said Easy! Nobody said Convenience! But here again is where a non-dualistic approach to work and play, love and hate becomes the only methodology.

As a Garter, I've learned from various Garter teachers, one of whom initiated me in certain Mysteries of Eros on the eve of my move to Las Vegas. After I told her about some of my general anxieties, she said, "The mind in its workings is crazy, the world in its workings is crazy. So the more you build up an indestructible sanctuary inside your soul, the more you can work with the crazy." Her suggestion for me was to cultivate "structure and devotion," two ways to fortify this sanctuary on a daily basis. (This Sanctuary notion, then, became an integral one in Garter practice and philosophy. Future dispatches and projects will involve how individual members can build up and cultivate their own Sanctuaries.) Much of this teacher's own work comes out of Sufi spirituality, Tibetan Buddhism and the Advaita Vedanta teachings of Shankara. For Garters, a major benefit of such spiritual work is the development in each individual soul of a taste for the pleasures of integration, and of submission to the energies of each day.

This conversation was one of the most revelatory of my life because of its jewel-like simplicity. Of course, its lessons have been difficult to uphold and yet they are always there as lanterns in the darkness. The Garters work separately and together to turn frustrations and disappointments into eerily-lit passageways; group work and group enthusiasm strengthen singular expeditions into the unknown. Later, in the desert, I realized that the unifying force of this sanctuary, the energy that fuses structure and devotion into committed reverential practice is Eros. This Eros is the love for the world in all its crazy manifestations but also a harder, more esoteric love that works with contradictions and complexities without trying to resolve them. The world, of course, tries, at every turn to dissuade us of this Love and this, too is an integral challenge of the path. The world, in all its fearful chattiness tries to inculcate us with the imperative that we must resolve things, tie up loose threads, establish rigorous limits and boundaries and reduce "negative" emotions and things in our lives. This world that instructs us thus is not at all the world that our bodies and souls live in, which is the world of opposing and clashing forces, of inhuman energies that don't always veer in our preferred directions.

Tantric practice echoes this in a similar fashion. According to Agehananda Bharati in *The Tantric Tradition*: "Reality is one, but it is to be grasped through a process of conceptual and intuitive polarization. The poles are activity and passivity, and the universe 'works' through their interaction." Thus, "self-love" becomes akin to the cultivating of a soul that is agile and generous enough to work with these polar energies. Instead of always seeking what is "similar," the soul learns to move among differences with fortitude, open-mindedness and, potentially, joy.

It has taken many blows, as they say, and wanderings, as well as many private joys, to grasp Eros as not just the range of ecstasies and agonies of romantic and sexual love but as a larger, more generous enchantment with the world's forces. At the same time, romantic and erotic love between entities can be a spiritual undertaking that releases creative and elemental energy, or constructs a "third mind" as William Burroughs and Brion Gysin call it. In this case, then, love is never "ideal," but instead is an imaginative leap into "real" energies that can seem alien and disorienting. This love can, in the words of a professor of mine, expand one's "available reality."

END BULLETIN

TREATISE ON THE "SACRED" TO BE QUESTIONED AND IMPLEMENTED IMMEDIATELY

If we are using the word "Sacred" does that mean we, the Garters, are a religious group?

Speaking for myself, merely one "member" of the Garters I will say this:

Foremost, it *implies* that I was probably raised (which I was) in a religious educational environment (Roman Catholic) and that early exposure to ideas or experiences of God and the sacred left indelible marks on me.

And they certainly did. One's childhood can never be overlooked or discredited. The Garters teach certain methods, however, to grasp childhood and infantile fixations, moments, forces and traumas—and alchemize them towards more joyous (and thus, more *potentiality-fueled*) expression. But my sense of the sacred was always bound up with the powers of art and language (the symbolic/creative realm) and also nature, even at its most suburban: its beauty, sublimity, alluring chasms, and sensory disorientations. The sacred then was felt most viscerally through *expressions*, whether of culture, nature, ritual, or their ambiguous intersections, and the transporting energies they entailed.

The world, Deleuze says, is nothing without its expressions. Do we accept this as a proposition for change, though, for the ongoing re-working of the "social imaginary"? As a teacher I ask my students this: how can we conceive of chaos and instability as a "good" thing? How do we express these parts of the real in affirmative terms?

Often, for me growing up, these were expressions of things that were difficult to express, verbalize or conceptualize, but the adventure of trying to do so was, itself, a rapturous and transformational occasion. And the sacred too was often experienced *through* transgressions of what my authorities had forbidden or rigidly demarcated. Transgression was a mode of expression that crossed boundaries or borders, imbuing my experience with transformational novelty, a confrontation with something Other. Often what was transgressed was something called "reason," which seemed to me a versatile concept tailored to the specific needs of whoever said the word with the most authority.

Here, the Sacred became closely allied with a concept of *Ecstasy*, as a necessary transport across levels of awareness, and as a method of refining consciousness in defiance of more restrictive and dogmatic psychic positionings. And I think that religion is one of very few realms where ecstasy, whether of the body, of thought, of the imagination, or whatever, is still revered as a necessary aspect of consciousness.

My feelings for the sacred/god/religious faith have gone through (and continue to) many permutations and subtleties, which tend to provoke more questions than answers, more strayings than certainties. Did it begin with the intensity of Catholic ritual, or with the feverish notes from my own, often, solitary imagination? Was it really there in the Transubstantiation of the Eucharist? Was it then complicated by the changes in my body, wherein desire and movement and Eros all pointed to other expressions of the Sacred? At some point too, a near-obsessive love for reading and writing entered the fray, in which the Sacred was equated with the possibility of a "new world," one which I could help create, participate in and share with others.

And yet there was no shock of illumination, or *satori* that I recall. No burst of light, or reverberations of angels. No smash on the head with a mallet as in certain Zen anecdotes. Violent enlightenment was not mine. But there was a gradual and subtle unfolding of images and tendencies, obsessions and suspicions, experiences and encounters that have led me to where I am today, to something that is, indeed a *calling* but that is also a *hearkening*, or a deep listening to all that has come before me and which echoes inside me.

So yes the Garters have religious tendencies insomuch as they are in love with and are bound to the invisible energies that animate this world.

But what do you mean by the Sacred?

I think "my sense of the Sacred" resides in the capacities, often latent or suppressed, of entities to *express* (and thereby embody, actualize, entail) some harmony (a beautiful integration of disparate parts) with the cosmos in its myriad, non-human energies, among its luminous differences, and throughout its dizzying, maze-like complexities. How such harmony is expressed and the intensities and transports of its manifestations, varies, and these variances obsess me as someone committed to expression. Whether or not "cosmos" is further equated with god, the divine or the numinous is also ground for rich discourse, as well as for many powerful aesthetic and devotional practices.

So then I would say, perhaps feebly, inadequately, that *the sacred*, as a term, connotes the presence of some imperishable and impenetrable vitality, or the sheer, indestructible *otherness* that illumines and animates the world in multifarious forms, and that would behoove us to be enchanted by, reverential towards and engaged with in thoughtful and complex ways. It is a force that is, at once, the most *archaic* and the most immediate; the most grounding and the most unsettling.

I may not always feel the Sacred as intently or naturally as I desire, or think I need to desire; or I may feel it only as something withheld by or suppressed by the powers that keep me busy and worried in a world largely composed of business and worry; or it may also be a lure that goads me down paths of research and exploration only to arrive back where I started, feeling even more beset by ambiguity. Whether it is all these things, or none, there remains the fact that It speaks. And I'm trying to listen as sincerely as I can.

How does the Body connect to the Sacred?

For the sake of a grounding provocation: We are daily robbed of our bodily potentials, transports and epiphanies. These primordial revelations are being obliterated by cultures that value hyper-rationality, attention deficit, the linear blows of Time, the amassing of material goods and superficial comforts and the reduction of any somatic, mental or emotional movements that are not purposeful or lucrative. When a student of the Garters becomes physically receptive to the Numinous and the Hyper-Speculative, she becomes more attuned to non-dualistic ways of being/becoming, which can be *initially* painful or unsettling passages to endure. But the intrepid Garter will eventually experiences a more ecological, and thus magical—to reassert an often naïve word—way of being in the world: we embody thru experience and empowerments the numerous strands and layers which compose our souls and which connect and diffuse them with others, whether human, animal, plant or netherwordly. This becomes a sensation of true wilderness entering in, and channeling/changing us. This voluminous Wild, whether it's urban or forested, coastal or mountainous is what we are after; it is the Garter Gnosis, the persisting of the Wild which we can ride upon, and among, without dissolution.

Often these primal explorations are unsettling or disarming because they ask you to realize the body as a laboratory of forces, spirits and vectors, to view the mind as a potentially fathomless realm of metamorphosis and to start viewing ritual, discipline, devotion and apprenticeship as not just part-time hobbies but unwavering commitments.

The Iron Garter must go against the grain of contemporary self-realization movements and self-commodification attitudes. There is no quick fixes or guaranteed ecstasies. There is no obsessing over your "profile" or "identity" to make it more exciting, appealing and ideal. In the terminology of Chogyam Trungpa, there are no "credentials" you can pin to your ego after a couple superficial sessions. You are asked to labor against these kinds of (also Trungpa's term) "spiritual materialisms" to reach the deeper radiances of the soul. Appearances aren't just superficial validations of ourselves nor are they anxiety-driven ornaments for the vanity of our egos, but instead they are pathways into deeper embodiments and transformations.

A Garter Precept is:
Appearance = Passage

Isn't this search for spiritual harmony a purely individualistic pursuit, a quest for self-actualization?

I think that this harmony is not and should not only be sought by individuals but also by groups, organizations, societies, states and whatever other social, erotic, spiritual and political assemblages can be imagined. The sacred, as I see it, is irreducible to dogma, fundamentalism, proscriptions of behavior, etc.; rather it is rooted in a tradition of differences, variously expressed and variously unfolding, which all feed from the same archaic source of Mystery and the resonances this Mystery unleashes on earth.

So I'm particularly interested in how the sacred can regain its influence in *political and social* formations (of diverse people, interests and affiliations), while hopefully undoing many of the tendencies that render politics so inimical to what is sacred. This is not asking for a dissolution of the barrier between church and state—for that is well under way in many nations already, with mixed results—but a more radically generous opening of the political realm to forces and entities that may seem alien to its "interests." That being said, the Garters, in their varied mobilizations strive to bring back the sacred into the social, but without the baggage of organized, fundamentalist religions.

Truly, the only "interests" that should be native to politics are the "real differences of and between beings," which is also the province, but through other rhetorics and methods, of certain religions. So it seems then, possibly, that religion and politics could, at some distant juncture be collapsed into a reverential practice of ecology—the harmonization of different expressions and entailments of being. The Garters are many things to many people, but among these manifestations they are the most agile unity of the sacred and the profane in a creatively political context.

But if you're really religious, you want to transcend this life, right? You live for an after-life or another world of being, right?

Some religious people do, certainly. But we Garters do not. We look at religion in its etymological origins: "reverence, vow, bind" and we understand the attitude we want to embody. It is indeed an attitude of reverence, an expression of a vow, and often a doubt-stricken, wavering vow at that– but a vow primarily to *this world* as the flowering of multifarious presence, and our own psyches as the vehicles through which this presence is intimately felt and through which it powerfully resounds.

This vow, however, does nothing on its own to directly combat my or your fears of annihilation, disorder, nothingness or the withdrawing of presence; but it may—and this is another motivation—lead us to methodologies through which such fears can be bravely met and benefited from, not just for my or your own life, but also for my or your life as it impacts and interacts with others. And these methods can be found in certain religious systems, just as they can be found in certain philosophical systems.

So yes, we believe that this pursuit of harmony, this intense intersecting with the Sacred is *not* a transcendence of the cosmic, material or earthly realms but a *deepening* of their beauty, presence, knowledge and radiance. Any sort of faith, for it to exist for us Garters, requires the unhampered, multi-faceted *expressions* of matter and the complex proliferations and intersections of what is alive, vital, mysterious and wondrous in the "here and now." It is also deeply rooted in a celebration of being «entity» in all its bodily profusions and frenzies which, themselves are often markers of the Sacred.

There is no withdrawing from the flux of creation, no restraining of the sensory faculties or pious distancing of myself from the constructions of the human imagination but, rather, there is a constant and rigorous refinement of how and why I engage with such beings and forces in the first place. It is a mode of attention that requires constant attention. Not everyone needs this mode of attention. Not everyone requires such refinements. In fact, such attentions and refinements exist outside of religious practice.

But uncountable bad things happen in This World all the fucking time.

Yes, and always will probably—but still, I at least have to recoil at notions of futurism, so-called accelerationism, the lust for interplanetary immigration or any kind of apocalyptic cynicism where the dying earth is abandoned, the historical nightmares finally exited. The "here and now," despite its incalculable miseries and injustices, its unsolvable ideological oppressions and inequities, and the ineradicable harms we have done to the earth, is also, in spite of our own human fears and prejudices, the flowering of the infinite expressions of entities as they interact with the living cosmos.

Living with a sense of the sacred, I think, is re-discovering daily this *newness* of the immediate earth, the fertile primacy of the living ground as it vibrates under the stars, the essential novelty and mystery of being conscious in a cosmos. It is to re-experience sensually, erotically, ethically and aesthetically a vibrant, sacred materialism flush with non-human and alien forces, all of which are native to the cosmos.

To abandon that process of expression and inquiry, to turn our backs upon this real ground of Mystery, to disown the symbolic and creative practices that are dependent upon the earth and its positioning in space-time, seems a cowardice, and a condemnation of any human experiment. Abandoning this process of stewardship—whose abandonment has reached an alarming rate anyway—seems then to be giving up on the mystery of being alive at all. More mystery = more devotion.

END BULLETIN

LOST LETTERS

FROM OUR OAKLAND, CALIFORNIA GARTER OPERATIVES

Letter one, Agent Q-76

Oakland docks: Never has obliteration & orgasm been so blended as in this struggle to keep dignified. I eat salted pineapple on scraped knees. Sun leaks bile thru the Pyramidal shipping containers. Someone keels over on the train-tracks. A force, from another, takes over my entire skin and I have no idea how I will live after. Dignity, the word is so attenuated I abhor its blithe abuses. Struggle too is defanged for whoever pays for it. I don't struggle as much as my neighbor, nor is my dignity as transparent as a child's. Words are no match for the writhing sensations that accompany them. Nothing involves us but the fragrant after burns.

Dignity, a word sells as candy, paired with news: technicality, decorum, armor. Nothing like mortar, or scabs has danced long with it. Right before I come, rampant in cayenne red, words inhere stranger entrails, I become a new kind of child. So I can handle dignity now having taken it into me,   then out of, something shapeable to give away.

Stranger's take on it is so pedantic as to be overheard in every office. We count the contraband feelings dignity refuses; then we refuse it.   We are the smuggled.

True dignity, a lover said, is *nostalgia for the present*—which, around here, we trick ourselves into feeling   our hands barbed from trying.

When we do feel it   she is right.   For now we drink blood oranges,   newly inked pamphlets, pirate radio in sunken beds,   cumin and lamb lard and rosemary shampoo   rubbed in friend's pits.

I will never believe I'm going to die today, get destroyed,   but likely a lover, cherished or forgotten, will take the plunge for me,   because of happenstance, which means this exactly: scaffolding, or ingrown fiascoes in how this game is rigged, but rigged more for some   than others.   *Fiasco*   is Italian for broken bottle, which is what our house floats on, what our sloppy heels get sliced on,   the word that enters us.

When I say lover I don't only mean bed-wreckers. But I certainly imply THAT and mazes more.   Nor is there just a profane &/or   cinematic way to   fuck.
Sky fucks thru this puissant glass, bathing its entities.   News fucks my sense of perspective, if I ever even had one.   When I come now, it is as violent as anything I've   never seen in the   movies.   I am never as true or clean or clear as my neighbor; or as crystalline as a child, but I know this, my fragments announce me, well in advance of their shadows   And as such…

They are a gift I can breathe thru the trash
and into you

Consider the implications, then make them work.

Dear Q,

Daily, I retreat further from the things that built me. I don't escape them though, just the twine that connects us gets so tangled up and eaten by other lines. If the other eight stowaways aren't already grumbling awake, they are after Henry makes his boisterous, Gene Kelly on angel dust entrance down the crumbling staircase. We start with nutmeg coffee out of a cracked French press and sticky buns that the bakery wanted to throw away. We complete our evenings with curry from the 99-cent store, honey-spiced ales and horror films, the combination conducive to nightmares that always hyperbolized some hysterical part of my trashcan adolescence.

By day, when we scamper around like work-dirtied bunnies, there are the delicious taco trucks and stealing from the pomegranate orchards of the slightly rich, down by Jack London. Or we splurge on Korean barbecue, which reduces us to vigilant catatonia, that pitch-perfect moment of Bachelardian day dreaming.

This last summer would get so stifling I took to sleeping outside on the concrete loading dock on a piece of factory-grade silk. Above me, an ochre moon hung like a pumice stone on the washboard of the Milky Way. My breasts were dirty and salt-crusted. My thighs scaled by unwashed tongues. And the whole of me was warm gold cooled by mortared dark. Cats, not as feral as the dogs would undulate out from the foliage as I slept, and keep me company, or else act threatening, when they were only having full-moon fevers. For this I forgave them, and we became inextricable on that exposed silk. Distant big-rigs, night police choppers, bleating of dogs, my own conjurations of future mayhem lulled me into a twisting and turning half-sleep among all that companionable fur and shard. Typically I find crumpled newspapers and a quiet park in the mornings. I read the names of the survivors on the plaque. The kids throw bottles at the lily-white joggers; the metal artists in their oil-stained Dickies score methadone behind the boarded-up church or liquor store. I try to adjust to the facts as they are given. Nothing moves how it is designed. But nobody can think of anything that works with everything there is. The whole of the Western part is industrial desert; all the buildings eroding back to their original scaffolding or jewel, the color of mildewed copper, tide pools, and rotting fruit. One word captures it: *ambergris.* Wednesdays, the parade of cement trucks broke the pre-dawn hush with the racket of churning and braking, backing-up and dumping. Evenings, we did our more daring runs. Rust was in. Old boat parts were in. Anything from a fire truck or an ambulance, a school bus or a golf cart. We didn't touch chemicals except a cheap cocktail of hash and opium, called Muppet Rock. I learned the wiles and bounties of broken-down machinery. What I learned I often repeated to you: in the breakages of dependable things are opportune chasms. No choice but to penetrate them. A crowbar or a composition book rarely left my satchel. Coffee could you drag out deep into the day, I discovered, and with water, turn you into a camel that could cross these industrial latitudes without cramping up or going hungry.

Dearest Zuq,

I open my aches up, let them call out to the others and follow my nose down the crumbling stairs. Our kitchen is just a bombed-out living room with improvised appendages. Yet this will be a template, mark my words. I am always hungry here but I learn to temper it through the wisdom found in the aches of others. Chosen sores are spigots you get a taste for, and then eventually a pungent wisdom that cannot be had by other, more sanitized faucets. I speak willfully vaguely, but you catch the drift. These are the conditions that have resisted us, now are us.

Gulls go begging right after dawn & our vaulted ceilings ripple in egg-shell blue as gilded dust dances in the corners. Doves or pigeons fatten their chests against the crusting glass. Such exhaling of the elements feels sacramental, for we all struggle to breathe as one living mosaic, and have to step on each other's sore or sharp points.

I always anticipate some explosive visitor from on high, an angelic paratrooper or a crash landing of a helicopter or guerrilla incubi. Instead I dream such visitations, almost nightly and experience their promised transformations between my legs.

Clouds in our home, slum-fecund, tinctured by the spirits of long-dead industry that never really dissipate, but only hibernate: oily dreams of cylinder merchants and tugboat conductors and peg-legged prostitutes, all of whom I've befriended just by walking towards them. In proximity is infrastructure.

I've watched old home movies of this neighborhood and our house-church still stands proudly in them, recalcitrant and dignified by brutality, amidst all the fallen buildings and collapsed freeways. But that earthquake should have obliterated us.

Multi-paneled cracked warehouse windows flood with sepia light as H. appears, like some punk-rock Liberace at the top of his own multi-colored, lopsided stairwell wearing polka-dot suspenders, shredded jeans dangling with army medals, and very little else. We are always half-naked around here, or our clothing increasingly takes on the tears, splotches, strands, gaping holes of action movie heroes and heroines. We consider the generic term "action," and how we can salvage it here, on the sidewalk, or in the walk-in closet, amongst all these molecules waiting to be jostled into radiance.

If we wore clothing proper, we'd be itching and going redder more than usual. Not from illness, but from weather that has been trapped here like some rare, ruby-backed moth.

I have to do something about the fractured headboard. I need to sweep the butterflies and sawdust away and buy bright orange tools, even if I don't use them. I made a note of all this on the back of a crumpled parking ticket as I slither into your underwear.

My Sweetest Corsair,

Thru gnats, sirens and vines, we slug down this frothing gorge, past plateaus of crocuses and oyster blue tombstones, where temples, festooned in candy paper lanterns, double as tombs, offices & altars, & Grasses coral, frond-tipped eat away rock faces; a cemetery crumbles upward into pines, just like the Civil War graves in Santa Cruz; on the summit sprawl unfinished construction sites of huge pipes, cinder blocks, half-lain foundations, calcified, sored in lichen, flapping with red, heraldic flags chewed up by Santa Anna winds....THIS breathless voyage! I am falling headlong into the conditions we invented. Alone & beset by words never once ever almost sufficient.

We don't tolerate that dime-store phrase: *ships in the night*. We voyage askance but distance and strangeness propose no real barriers. Space is never as terminal as we portend. The flesh has handholds in a tempest. We are parallel vessels at all hours, always vibrating, forever relaying, pinging, volleying: piratical courtship across latitudes and narrows. Foam kicked up in your wake finds a way to my eyelids. It matters little in courtly love on the run if the courted is conscious of being pinged. The darts land below the gossip-churning mind, in the surface's depths, where chatter grows encrypted, and thus fertile.

You fertilize me & I you: thru code, veiled in distance.

You boarded the *Elsewhere*, pariah vessel in *Dogpatch* sludge basins. The burly old Dodge was a versatile dry dock. But for you, all this earth flows, in smuggled tributaries under shopping malls. The hurried notes you sent left me euphoric. Even though I had grown mute and dispersed. For your work was nuancing, growing as spectral as the games of the sand mystics: you had carved *portals* all over the mainland, turned the kids into experimental cosmonauts, and seeded the *crypts* with numinous and violet portents.

We must traverse these unendurable coordinates, you conclude—which is why I spit into paper, blabber at structures, lose trousers with no incentives. When I taste raw calcite, I feel your lashes pivot off a cypress-browed moon. You explain your cartographic methods as I melt away. The muddy night after crashing the canoe, we had nothing but macadamias to eat and only slick, sheer promontories to gorge ourselves on.

But this is why we boarded a ship in the first place: to know that distance is traversable and goes quite green, even with gathering darkness. I look forward to being disappointed because I'll know then I'll still be going. I've attached a totemic picture of our hinterlands.

TRESPASSIONS

MAIL ART
AND THE SEMINAL INFLUENCES
OF
GENESIS P-ORRIDGE

I was in New Orleans in 2004, staying with my girlfriend in a former brothel turned hotel that had termites gnawing the bedposts. Strange hieroglyphic carvings shone on the hardwood floor of our red and cavernous room. I imagined they were codes incised by century-old stiletto heels, an improvised vernacular you could decipher like hobo signs. We spent an evening admiring the poison bottles—gorgeously blue and multi-sided—inside the haunted pharmacy museum. We encountered the famous fake saint of New Orleans, "St. Expedite," the patron of quick solutions, sailors and schoolboys. Such idol worship thrilled us; what could be made-up could also be made real. And what was real could always be recontextualized at a moment's notice.

My girlfriend was an artist making sculptures of imaginary organs. I was writing stories about cults and border towns. I had packed a single book for that short trip: the glossy, illustrated *Painful but Fabulous: The Lives and Art of Genesis P-Orridge*. In between cemeteries, ghost tours, antique shops and smoky little dive bars full of church pews

ADAPTED AND EXPANDED FROM AN ARTICLE PUBLISHED AT THE *RUMPUS*, SAN FRANCISCO, SPRING 2013 and stained glass, I read the book with an ever-increasing exhilaration each time I opened it. In the welter of New Orleans, *Painful but Fabulous* acted like hormonal propaganda on my impressionable twenty-three-year-old brain. Through interviews and appreciations, manifestos and collages, the book tells how Genesis pioneered many strange cultural eruptions, from industrial music to body modification, mail art to performance art, cut-up writing to "chaos magic," modern primitivism to techno and on and on. He realized early that our human experience was mired in mystery and that art, music, ritual and provocation could make him a medium of this very mystery. Art as an evolving force had consumed his life, and his art changed as psychic and social conditions changed. This ever-questioning, ever-mutable culture existed as a challenge to rigid, consensus culture, or so the story went, even when the latter often co-opted the former.

After reading *Painful but Fabulous*, I knew I had to become more committed to my own artistic and creative goals. If I wanted to be a full-time writer and artist, I needed discipline as a weapon against the world's titanic indifference, as well as my own internalized blockages. I had the endless curiosity of a dilettante but not the tenacious work habits of Genesis who once declared, "You should always aim to be as skillful as the most professional of government agencies. The way you live, conceive and market what you do should be as well thought out as a government coup. It's a campaign, it has nothing to do with art." What I feared was that I would give up my creative goals simply to meet the biological and social demands of survival and comfort, status and convenience.

Back in San Francisco, daily life resumed: we needed to pay rent, find a new roommate, do mountains of laundry, cook relatively healthy meals. I went back to work at a construction company, answering phones and printing up reports eight hours a day. I had more or less accepted the inevitable: with my literature degree, a clean, well-lighted office desk was my fate. I realized, at the same time, I was one of thousands of creative types who had come into a similar fate. After all, I was a member of that entitled and naïve generation of over-encouraged children who get liberal arts degrees and expect the world to come leaping into their laps. Or at least that was how the media liked to hyperbolize my own admittedly naïve optimism about life.

I was congenial and humorous enough to calm down our clients and meticulous enough to stamp every envelope that required one. Yet the job was monotonous, completely uninspiring and overrun by boorish superiors. Nor was my desk clean or well-lighted: I picked rat droppings off my keyboard every morning and had to wipe sawdust and dead insects off the windows every afternoon. The floor of my office was made of rotting plywood that I often stepped through. Between filth and tedium, I was struggling to justify the work beyond my mediocre paycheck.

I was baffled by the value put on waste in office work. (I would retain this awe when I later worked in brokerage, architecture and law firms, as I was forever implicated in a paper trail that led nowhere but the recycling bin or the shredder.) I was trying to think artistically about my work which to me seemed more practical than ever. How could I redeem these wasted minutes performing wasteful (and wasted) tasks? Even while the work just barely paid my bills I had to make it work for me on an entirely different level. At least art could transform so much meaninglessness.

Taking my cue from Genesis, I started creating "mail art" on the clock, using all the anachronistic machines we made our boring reports with: heat-binders, laminators, giant hole-punchers, etc. These machines existed to churn out lavish and supremely unnecessary technicalities that would be destroyed or filed away forever the moment they arrived. At least my art would reach someone, I told myself—in this case, my girlfriend who would receive the mail at our apartment. My dispatches were mostly typed on the computer and instantly deleted once they were printed up. If I had done my assigned work and spent the rest of my hours sunk in daydreams, there would have been no proof I had actually lived out those on-the-clock minutes. But now I was creating a real paper trail that led to a real person and a real made-up world that we held in common and sustained.

I wrote reports of my lunchtime rambles down seedy 6th Street where I often ate rice vermicelli at the counter of the Vietnamese dive *Tu Lan* while chatting with day traders or journalists or social workers. Knowing that I would rush back to my work computer and write about it, I peeled my eyes for things I might otherwise disregard: colorful heaps of trash, hidden murals, men playing chess, people leaning out of SRO windows, mangled books on the ground. The anticipation of writing made my half-hour lunches much more intriguing. I described the furniture factories, porn shops, donut stores and liquor stores of the South of Market area in minute detail. Often I would find weird, faded flyers on the ground and include them, whole or cut-up, in my letters. A whole ramshackle microcosm was showing itself in my writing, a world of artisans and drifters, day-drinkers and prostitutes, leather daddies and junky bakers, Laundromat custodians and car window smashers. These were the people I wanted to know about, in life and in fiction, in daydreams and in myth.

Once, my manager almost caught me with a hastily written pornographic story that I had pulled hot off the shared printer. A lot of what I wrote was sexually explicit and adorned with brazen heirlooms of my sex life with my girlfriend. The landscape of Soma with its used condoms in the alleys and sex shops and leather bars reflected and refracted my own desires. Nothing was more exciting than injecting the dull workday with the intimate mementos of my "private" life. But I evaded capture and the result became six months' worth of daily mail: false reports, found objects, collages, poetic rants and obscenity-laden letters that I mailed to our apartment, ephemera that I'm still mining for inspiration.

The extra half hour to an hour I devoted every day to my art in no way compromised my actual work performance. I did more than my assigned duties (and did them well, my manager claimed) and had time leftover for my own "work." It was one way of dealing with oppressive labor: by infiltrating it with a parallel story. The fact that it was done secretly only enriched the excitement. If something seemed dull and purposeless, you could covertly make it thrilling. Injecting the job with a secondary and secretive purpose also invested the necessary job minutiae (paper clips, stamps, lunch breaks, bathroom breaks) with freshly mysterious significance. Work life would never be the same because I had developed the imaginative tools to subvert it.

Imagination is the filter that alchemizes experience. But it is also an infection, a bundle of kindling and an intensively virulent vector. Art *defamiliarizes* things and this is also a survival strategy. If we're overly familiar with the mechanistic tedium that dictates our minutes we might not persist in attending to them. (Things get dicey in the current enterprise and entrepreneurial economies where "imagination" and "creativity" are touted by suits in every possible banality. How do we engage with this? How do we make creativity a secret force again?)

So the process is just as important and interesting and exciting as any outcome. I've had several office jobs since that construction company in which I've performed dull, repetitive tasks for a paycheck. Alone this makes me like everybody else, probably. But I still believe that wonder and humor can be mined from even the most banal work conditions. The whole process I went through in making mail art at work was a good way of awakening what Genesis calls "the third mind" (borrowing a term from h/er mentors William Burroughs and Brion Gyson): "by juxtaposing or clashing two minds, objects, phenomena, thoughts, feelings… new ideas and inspirations occur." There are many moments in life when survival and security demand that you take boring things seriously. But you can redeem the dullness and counteract the monotony, sometimes by imagining a wildly different story about it. A wild and different story that can be as true as the ones you are made to believe.

END BULLETIN

LOST
IN THE
ARCHIVES

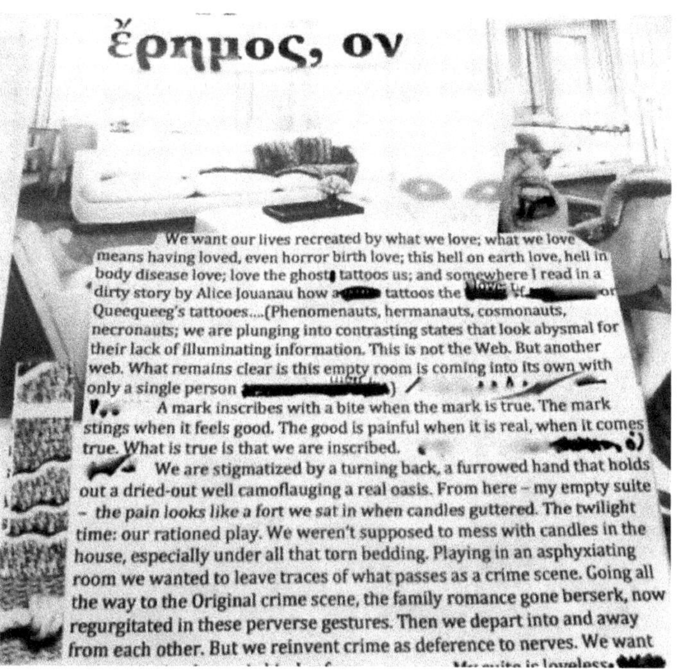

AGENT CORRESPONDENCES · SAN FRANCISCO, OAKLAND, LAS VEGAS, 2004–2015

"Hi M

in this time of coincidences, I felt I had to send you a line. My name is Emma and I am writing from Berlin.

This morning I went on-line looking for a quote by John Berger. In my search I ended up reading part from your blog dated Oct. 21th 2009.

There you write about how you found a beautiful edition of "To the wedding", in which you had found the Brassai card. The same card sits on the bulletin board over my desk and was given to me as a birthday card from my friend Klara.

A couple of days ago, on Oct. 21 to be exact, I visited Klara in Copenhagen and spent the night at her place. As I had brought nothing to read, she handed me "To the wedding" as a bed-time read. I was surprised and delighted that she handed me this very book, as I had been giving Bergers "Ways of Seeing" to my students in spatial composition at the Danish Theatre School the same afternoon.

I had first discovered "Ways of Seeing" as it was left behind in my apartment by another friend who stayed at my place when I was in San Francisco a couple of years ago. It now sits in my bookshelf, coincidentally surrounded by two novels by M. Oondatje, who you also write about, reflecting on Berger.

I thought that all of this was too remarkable not to notice and share.

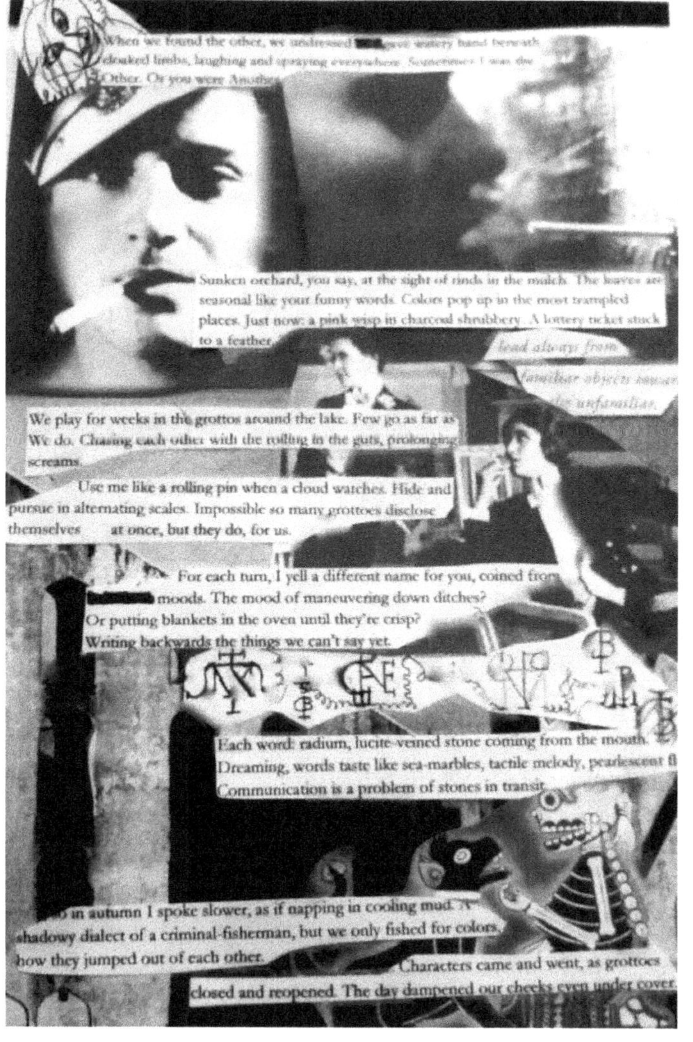
When we found the other, we undressed watery hand beneath
cloaked limbs, laughing and spraying everywhere. Sometimes I was the
Other. Or you were Anoth
Sunken orchard, you say, at the sight of rinds in the mulch. The leaves are
seasonal like your funny words. Colors pop up in the most trampled
places. Just now: a pink wisp in charcoal shrubbery. A lottery ticket stuck
to a feather.
lead always from
familiar objects
unfamiliar.
We play for weeks in the grottos around the lake. Few go as far as
We do. Chasing each other with the rolling in the guts, prolonging
screams.
Use me like a rolling pin when a cloud watches. Hide and
pursue in alternating scales. Impossible so many grottoes disclose
themselves at once, but they do, for us.
For each turn, I yell a different name for you, coined from
moods. The mood of maneuvering down ditches?
Or putting blankets in the oven until they're crisp?
Writing backwards the things we can't say yet.
Each word: radium, lucite-veined stone coming from the mouth.
Dreaming, words taste like sea-marbles, tactile melody, pearlescent
Communication is a problem of stones in transit.
in autumn I spoke slower, as if napping in cooling mud. A
shadowy dialect of a criminal-fisherman, but we only fished for colors,
how they jumped out of each other.
Characters came and went, as grottoes
closed and reopened. The day dampened our cheeks even under cover.

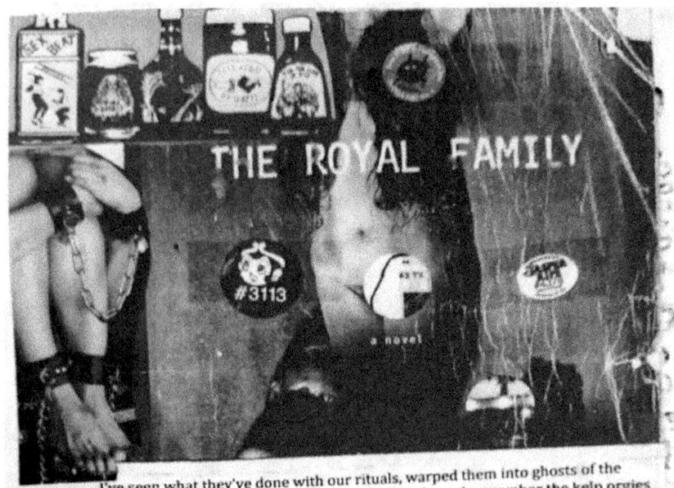

I've seen what they've done with our rituals, warped them into ghosts of the original spasms. Take these binder clips and rubber bands, and remember the kelp orgies and vine fires of a life before offices and cities, when the sand erased distinctions. I raise the pen to my teeth, as they do. Like them I am strange only If I think about it.

TRESPASSIONS UNLIMITED
c/o M. BALTHAZAR de COVERLY
674 HAIGHT ST. APT. 2
SAN FRANCISCO, CA
94117

THE
IS ESPE
POWERFU

We come, of course, from different precincts. Can't quite believe it, can you! How the two of us, with the ease of incest, mated under a darkling tree owned by the Government.

Funny to relive it here while I'm making a Kilimanjaro of photocopies to be destroyed in a distant shredder.

There were super malls and car wrecks. Boutique candy stalls misted in cherry smoke. Nothing like the boxed greyness of the present.

I tried to explain the Lake to the Boss today.

But he was wondering aloud about the efficacy of having my desk facing the wall or the window. But the window is on the wall, I said. But suppose the wall is in the window? he joked. Downstairs, the men cook meat disastrously close to the extracted hulls.

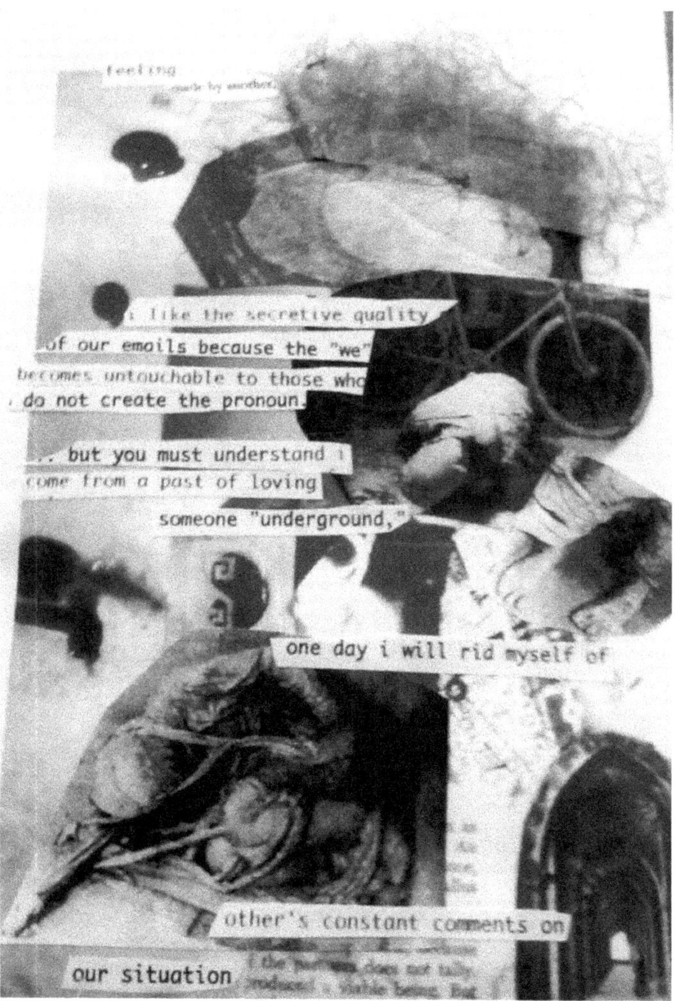
feeling
i like the secretive quality
of our emails because the "we"
becomes untouchable to those who
do not create the pronoun.
... but you must understand i
come from a past of loving
someone "underground,"
one day i will rid myself of
other's constant comments on
our situation

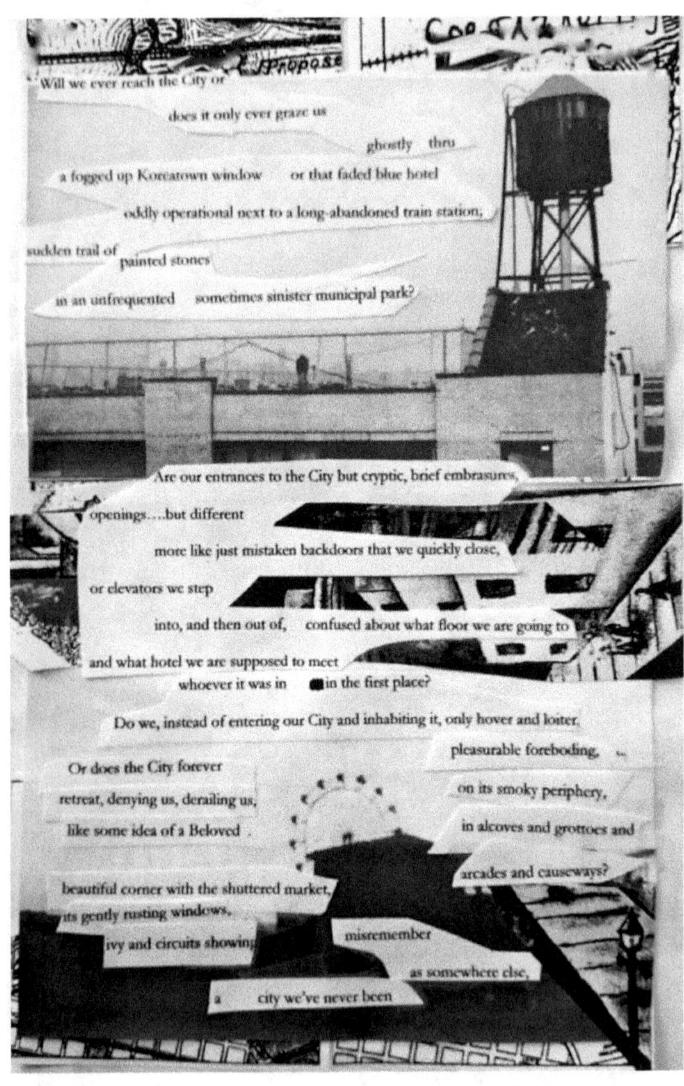
Propose
Will we ever reach the City or
does it only ever graze us
ghostly thru
a fogged up Koreatown window or that faded blue hotel
oddly operational next to a long-abandoned train station,
sudden trail of painted stones
in an unfrequented sometimes sinister municipal park?
Are our entrances to the City but cryptic, brief embrasures,
openings....but different
more like just mistaken backdoors that we quickly close,
or elevators we step
into, and then out of, confused about what floor we are going to
and what hotel we are supposed to meet
whoever it was in in the first place?
Do we, instead of entering our City and inhabiting it, only hover and loiter.
pleasurable foreboding,
on its smoky periphery,
in alcoves and grottoes and
arcades and causeways?
Or does the City forever
retreat, denying us, derailing us,
like some idea of a Beloved
beautiful corner with the shuttered market,
its gently rusting windows,
ivy and circuits showing
misremember
as somewhere else,
a city we've never been

THE GIFT AND THE MESSAGE

NOTES, TESTIMONIES, UNSENT BULLETINS ON COMMUNICATION, TECHNOLOGY, MESSAGING AND THEIR DISCONTENTS

The Garters are becoming less interested in relying on screens as their main interface with others. We say this but our actions betray it. Even now, if our phone makes a sound, we lunge for it and see what message, if any awaits us. Machines make us compulsive. We have become trained and tamed by our tools. But this is not how we want to be at all. Instead, we want to use screens when they are practical and accommodating, but we also want more varied, even *stranger* modes of sending and receiving messages. Moreover, we don't want to habitually discount the "outside world," which, we propose, is the world that is not completely contained by a screen. We are not interested in reducing the textures and mysteries of the outside to what blips, beeps and ticks upon a screen. If being a messenger is a role we take seriously, we must expand our options, or consider new and undreamt ones. The Iron Garters are messengers but the messages they secrete are not always the most convenient, legible or validating ones; instead, they are composed of mystery, which is what still, when all is stripped away, composes life itself.

UNSENT BULLETINS · LAS VEGAS, WINTER 2014

A footnote that came unmoored

[1] "My darling, what is the Message then? How is it now that we are forever awaiting messages, even the most inconsequential ones and even the truly surprising ones? We have learned that surprises can have their harbingers once we have been messaged enough times. We want mystery to endure, but only in allurement, is that right? We want to be allured but never to the abyss? I wonder what primal scenes are tangled up in *my own crypt.* I want to say that you make me more patient, which means, I think more attentive to what is unbreachable. But also the word "angel" comes from the word "envoi" or "messenger" and to me this suggests that—"

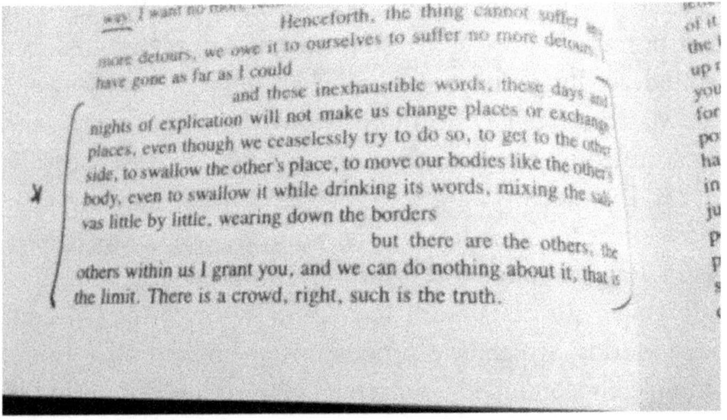
Henceforth, the thing cannot suffer more detours, we owe it to ourselves to suffer no more detours, have gone as far as I could

and these inexhaustible words, these days and nights of explication will not make us change places or exchange places, even though we ceaselessly try to do so, to get to the other side, to swallow the other's place, to move our bodies like the other's body, even to swallow it while drinking its words, mixing the saliva little by little, wearing down the borders

but there are the others, the others within us I grant you, and we can do nothing about it, that is the limit. There is a crowd, right, such is the truth.

We spent a lot of time with this really beautiful, frustrating and moving Derrida book, *The Post Card* in the Las Vegas spring (excerpted above). ⅓ of the book (called "Envois") consists of "partially destroyed imaginary letters" Derrida writes to his unnamed, distant beloved. (Seeing as we're big fans of letters, love letters especially and anything to do with mail, post offices, care packages, stamps, etc., this book definitely *seduces directly.*) Many of these imagined letters riff on Plato, Socrates, Freud, Heidegger, etc., but all within the context of this feverish, displacing, torturous love he feels towards this Other who is never quite present or "available." They are always missing each other (via badly-timed letters, trains, cars and telephone calls), never quite flush with one another; always out-swerving the other, causing havoc to each one's semi-illusory equilibrium, and their reality is only accountable through this obsessive paper trail they each secrete. The fact of *not* arriving becomes almost more significant, more charged and more seductive than those planned moments of nexus or connection. Arrival, in itself becomes what is to be avoided. And throughout Derrida manages to make several risqué, scatological punning jokes on Socrates and Plato (who are immortalized in a bizarre postcard (of the book's title) that Derrida finds in a junk shop.) For all its heavy-handed ardor, the book is often quite hilarious and only strengthens my notion that Derrida is one of the funnier theorists around.

The book viscerally captures the repetition and the compulsiveness of communication: this apparent accumulation of data, opinion, sensation and feeling which never quite add up to anything more eloquent than a cry or a moan, and the haunting insistence on being both disjointed and fused with the Other, forever in mid-swerve, always-already out of step, never not vigilant for implosion or dispersal or vertigo even when in repose—I think we who have loved or crushed or courted can pretty much relate. The book overflows with memorably heated fragments, almost like theory-poetry, like the above, which I randomly found this morning on my phone as I was deleting photos. Plus it makes you consider, from many unconsidered angles, just what is at stake in any relationship, or love, or relation.

For me what's at stake is that being human means, among other things being a messenger; thus my responsibility is to learn what messages I want to disseminate in the world, to the ones I love and to the ones I know nothing about; likewise, what messages will I pick up, take in and remix in myself from the world, from Others, to send back out to the world?

So pivoting off that assumption, in the spring I used Derrida's book for an essay on love, the unknown, online dating and what, possibly, adventure means, especially when people say they "like adventure" in their online dating profiles. In the original essay, I ended up advocating for a broader, more eclectic and stranger spectrum of communication and messages between individuals—but I think my reasoning was esoteric and/or humorous and/or deliberately provocative at best. Basically I was saying: don't fear the illegible, because the heart doesn't (the heart *requires* it) *and* likewise not everything that is revealed is profound.

But still I acknowledge my enormous debt to the Internet for multiplying opportunities for so-called adventure and traffic with the Unknown. For Tumblr, OKCupid, Facebook, MySpace, Friendster have certainly invited wonderful and illuminating people, moments, fiascoes, mysteries, mishaps and joys into my life I probably wouldn't have found otherwise.

But we shouldn't limit our capacities as messengers to these mediums. Nor should we limit our ability to receive messages to what blips and beeps on a screen.

A preference for legibility tends to replicate messengers who *only* deliver legibility, i.e. what is already recognizable, replicable and so inherently contagious. Risks, surprises and detours become instantly curtailed, or at least become harder to uncover. What is *strange* and *other* will become policed into banal recognition without anyone the wiser. A *meme* is exemplary of this phenomenon. What you see *is* what you see, and you can ping it along indefinitely, with slight nuances and variations. The best thing about adventure and the unknown, I also semi-concluded is that, befitting their literal meanings, we'll never quite understand either one, or exhaust either one, or prepare thoroughly for either one. We can only, with a reasonable amount of fear and positive expectation enter into them like the questing humans that we are.

And once immersed in them, we might not even know that we are, nor be able to report back on our experiences until much later, when our very words and minds have already altered and are hastily creating a retroactive commentary at many removes from what actually happened. For whose to say at what point the unknown becomes knowable, or even simply reportable; or similarly when does adventure become misadventure, or, more broadly, when are we ever not venturing? When does life cease being a venture and simply something ordinary that is happening?

It is telling though how "Adventure" has become quite a buzz word in people's online identities. You would think that if you went to all the trouble of making an online dating profile that you intend on curbing the severely adventurous aspects of dating, like what happens often, for instance, when you meet strangers out in the "real world." But "adventure" is supposed to read as "exciting," kind of like listing "travel" as an interest means you are probably "adventurous" and "open-minded" and "worldly." More than anything, we don't want to seem boring, even if, potentially, "boredom" is the biggest adventure of all, because it is an occasion when we are absolutely at the mercy of the unknown, and, thus, our own riled imaginations.

We long for and we need narratives; Joan Didion told us that, and it's true. With love, especially, we need to feel we are a part of an unfolding logic. Love retroactively constructs a timeline, along with a complete archive of messages of variable import, accuracy and intent. It is said that the first six months of any love affair is a milieu where all messages are provocative *and* effective. Whoever first said that to me made that generalization become a commandment. How often the opinions of others pierce us this way! Derrida says that the origins of the word *archive* come from both *commencement* and *commandment*: you are thus compelled to create an archive, which induces a juridical violence... and organizational violence.

My fellow Garter, I do not want to generalize on our first six months because they are peculiarly plotted, wildly tangential, sensually haphazard and resist the spatiotemporal logic of the romantic narratives I am used to hearing. We don't live in the same city for instance, but we have made love in five states, and yet we have only spent about 25 days together total over an entire year than began on a whimsical trip to ________. Not to mention the fact that I met you in a dark place my first night in ________ when, prompted by fatigue, travel and exile, and the way the candlelight spattered your face in that cavernous bar, I went up to you and said something stupid but *NOT that* stupid it turns out. (The vernacular today posits our encounter as *strange*—but we know the connotations of this are demeaning to the woman involved in the encounter.)

Yet I hold in my hands nine letters you have now written me, one that included a ___________, per my ebullient request, which made you, I was glad to hear, even more ebullient. In *The Post Card*, this book I will begin to tell you about, Derrida engages in an incessant play of reminders, reenactments, reassertions, reinvestments in oscillating degrees of clarity and lyricism, as a method, I think of *disseminating* romance. There is, in romance, a transformation of the message into that which cannot arrive. It becomes hard to think about clearly without turning away from it.

An unincorporated unsent letter: "Stories, if you can call them that, (but for convenience's sake what else can I call them?) like *this* one of *Us*, dash back and forth and sideways in space, time, psyches, and so dismantle their status as story in the process. But the narrative logic simplifies; it has to necessarily to present itself legibly.

Is what we're doing legible to anyone else? Is it even legible to us? I think we encrypt each other through our messages, through the feelings, of hesitation or nervousness that might arise if we don't respond or reply in an as effusive or timely manner as the other. For instance, in deference to narrative logic, someone (typically a chump) might say *we* (us) privilege letters over emails because we are quaint, nostalgic, fetishizing anachronism. Letters came before email, just like Derrida rifts on Socrates coming before Plato and vice versa; and how this sequencing is illusory yet highly structural at the same time. Nobody but charlatans have disputed that illusion is inherently structural. But then nobody has yet demarcated either where or whether illusion ends. Although I guess, to be fair: that is only four types of messages (email, phone call, text message, letters). I wonder though what messages we are *not* indulging in? How can we message or ping each other in a way that preserves a subtlety, obliqueness, that irresistible swerving/drift that is one with pure seduction? Because of my unflinching romanticism (a composite of books and experiences) I posit that romance must retain the mystery of its inauguration even if one must resort to hermetic and obscure methods, i.e. to play that disrupts and derails. I wonder how too soon we say things that could stand to be said much later. I imagine a most patient interloper, using all the words at her behest, who operates by a more esoteric grammalogical timetable. When I hypothesize all the time, you must understand I am not accusing you of doing the opposite of these hypotheses,

I'm only suggesting that difference is traversable and that oppositions themselves can be curtailed or at least rendered irrelevant.

HermEros and the *Necronauts*: The Seeds of a New Collaboration

The Iron Garters are pursuing clandestine border-work but in the realm of Eros, especially through Her vigorously policed and encrypted Hermetic (i.e. Hermes, communication) emanations. We are obsessed with the deferrals of Eros, the tangents, breakdowns, vortices and fractures that seed new events and divergent types of messengers and messages. Much of the work in this field, which we dub HermEros is inspired by an indirect and oblique dialogue with the art group called the INS. The cross-genre, philosophical, conceptual and artistic work undertaken by the *International Necronautical Society*, especially in their provocative reports collected in *The Mattering of Matter* are inspired by Derridean notions of absence, *différance* and dissemination.

Here's more on them: "Founded in 1999 by Tom McCarthy, the International Necronautical Society (INS) spreads itself as both fiction and actuality, often blurring the two. Famously described as "replaying the avant-garde along the faultline of death" (*Art Monthly*, London), the INS inhabits and appropriates a variety of art forms and cultural 'moments' from the defunct avant-gardes of the last century to the political, corporate and conspiratorial organisations they mimicked. The INS's manifestos, proclamations, reports, broadcasts, hearings, inspectorates, departments, committees and sub-committees are the vehicles for interventions in the space of art, fiction, philosophy and media." —from the INS website, http://necronauts.net/manifestos/1999_transcript.html

Since death is a sort of impossible/possible absence,

"necronauts" devote their labors to surveying Death's border regions: "If the INS sees death from a spatial and geographical point of view, the primary task of its agents is to patrol the border zones, like Cold War spies operating on both sides of the Iron Curtain" (preface, *Mattering*, 15).

Death invites suggestive deflections, deferrals and encryptions of meaning, many of which can be used to disrupt notions of ideality and legibility. More often than not, the unexplored region of death can only send back noise, or, in Derridean terms, "traces" that need to be unscrambled and decoded. The trick, for any good *necronaut* (which all of us, being mere mortal already are) is to construct a "craft" that can weather this vague navigation through often insensible or impenetrably encrypted matter. Artists and philosophers are the best-equipped to endure this navigation, as their perceptions are already skewed towards *ostranenie.*

Like Tom McCarthy, the INS General Secretary, and Simon Critchley, the INS Chief Philosopher, the Iron Garters are inspired by researches into communication performed by Jacques Derrida (especially in his book, *The Post Card*). However, we will also introduce a few not insignificant swerves, by excavating the fractured libidinal archives of online dating and social media sites (and its generative hilarities, intrigues and deflections) as an exemplary social media site for our erotic and hermetic inquiries. Soon, we will inaugurate an Iron Garters Cryptic Media Site which induces its select participants to engage in real-world adventures and initiations.

In Derrida's introduction to *The Wolf Man's Magic Word* by Nicolas Abraham and Maria Torok he considers what Torok and Abraham are evoking in the psychoanalytic term, *crypt:* "a *safe*: sealed, and thus internal to itself, a secret interior within the public sphere, but, by the same token, outside it, external to the interior" (foreword, *The Wolf Man,* xiv). In true Derridean terms, interiors and exteriors are conflated and dispersed by the use of this term, *crypt*. He is inquiring, as well, what is possessive *within* the self's interiority and what, by being decrypted, can be released from this possessiveness. What the crypt and its verbal markers, or *cryptonyms* seem to suggest is that "encryption generates desire and desire generates encryption" (*The Mattering of Matter*, 193). Although the "refusal to mourn" is an indication of the existence of a psychic *crypt*, the deflection from this tendency becomes, instead a broadcasting of desire (ibid., 194). Shame, too, is constitutive of crypts, especially in the case of The Wolf Man (whose story involves incest, animal torture, and anal eroticism, among other markers). Wherever libidinal energy surges, the threatening marker of shame is not far off—and current technology knows this!

Encrypted or not, desire, when hearkened, can also call us "outside" of possessive interiority and cajole us to exteriorize our own neuroses, fixations, and *cathexes* in fractured forms that drift into and among other forms. What we are saying is that desire makes us into artists, which are the most versatile of messengers. And this is the realm where Messages become Angelic again, or initiatory.... But the *initiatory* power of messages has almost entirely been lost in these considerations, in deference to practical, and infinitely replicable/memed messages. To invite types of messages that initiate its receiver into the unknown is to invoke and deliberately call in the "strange," or that which is wildly exterior to our reasonable expectations. How could we acknowledge the Unknown when or if we were pinged/messaged by it? Only by deferral, displacement, or a flood of ambiguity that often leaves us ____________________.

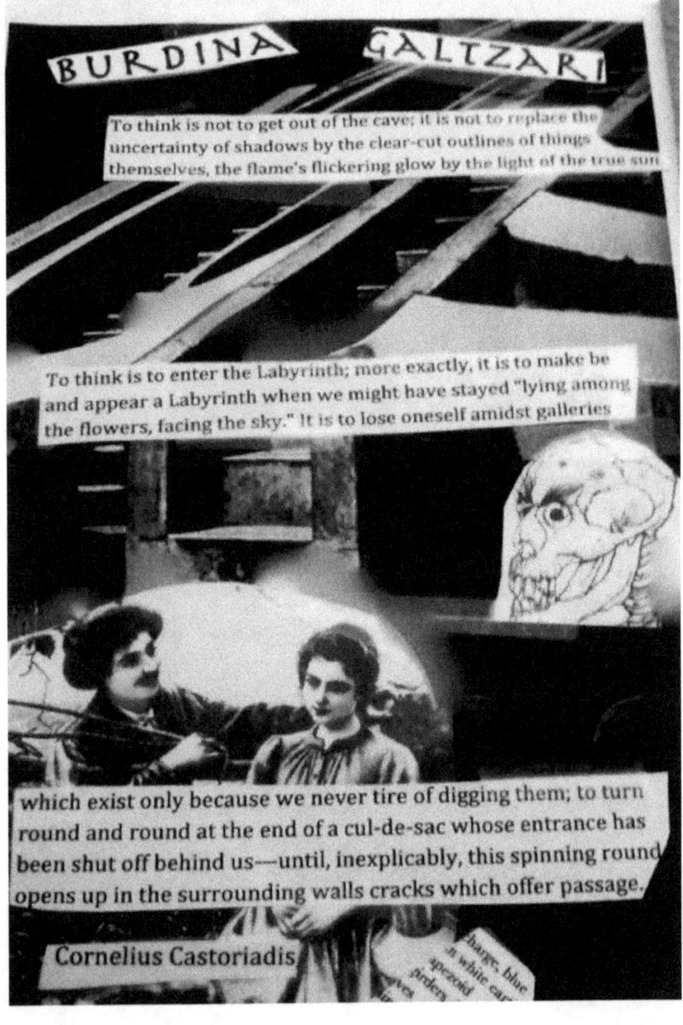
BURDINA GALTZARI
To think is not to get out of the cave; it is not to replace the
uncertainty of shadows by the clear-cut outlines of things
themselves, the flame's flickering glow by the light of the true sun
To think is to enter the Labyrinth; more exactly, it is to make be
and appear a Labyrinth when we might have stayed "lying among
the flowers, facing the sky." It is to lose oneself amidst galleries
which exist only because we never tire of digging them; to turn
round and round at the end of a cul-de-sac whose entrance has
been shut off behind us—until, inexplicably, this spinning round
opens up in the surrounding walls cracks which offer passage.
Cornelius Castoriadis

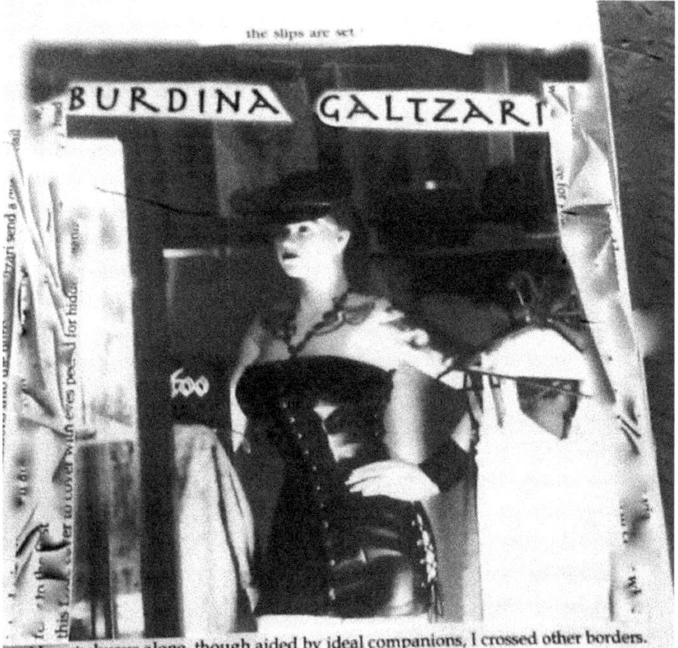
the slips are set
BURDINA GALTZARI
Almost always alone, though aided by ideal companions, I crossed other borders. My emotion was always equally great. I crossed Alps of all kinds. From Slovenia to Italy, helped by the customs men, then abandoned by them, I went upstream, along a muddy torrent. Fought by the wind, by the cold, by the thorns, by November, I gained a summit behind which was Italy. In order to reach it I affronted monsters hidden by the night or revealed by it. I got caught in the barbed wire of a fort where I heard the sentinels walking and whispering. Crouching in the shadow, my heart beating, I hoped that before shooting me they would fondle and love me. Thus I hoped that the night would be peopled by voluptuous guards.
—Jean Genet, The Thief's Journal

END

THE
IRON GARTERS
INAUGURAL
ARCHIVE

SECOND VOLUME
PENDING?

www.ingramcontent.com/pod-product-compliance
Lightning Source LLC
La Vergne TN
LVHW010628100826
845148LV00014B/3155

* 9 7 8 0 6 9 2 2 8 3 9 5 0 *